Decision Making for Personal Investment

Waymond Rodgers • Timothy G. McFarlin

Decision Making for Personal Investment

Real Estate Financing, Foreclosures and Other Issues

palgrave
macmillan

Waymond Rodgers
University of Texas, El Paso/
University of Hull
Hull, United Kingdom

Timothy G. McFarlin
McFarlin LLP
California, USA

ISBN 978-3-319-47848-7 ISBN 978-3-319-47849-4 (eBook)
DOI 10.1007/978-3-319-47849-4

Library of Congress Control Number: 2016957407

Printed on acid-free paper

This Palgrave Macmillan imprint is published by Springer Nature
The registered company is Springer International Publishing AG
The registered company address is: Gewerbestrasse 11, 6330 Cham, Switzerland

Preface

Personal investments generally involve one's current needs as well as predicting one's long-term requirements, which an individual/family performs to spend monetary resources taking into consideration various financial risks. These investments can take the form of checking, savings accounts, stock market, bonds, and mutual funds. Also, other vehicles can be utilized such as credit cards, consumer loans as well as insurance (life insurance, health insurance, disability insurance) and individual-/employer-sponsored retirement plans, social security benefits, and income tax management.

Nonetheless, many individual investors simply do not have the tools to cope with financial decisions or they are constrained by circumstances (such as time pressure, changing environments, ill-structured information, and lack of expertise regarding financial issues) or the information is just too much.

In our fast-moving economy we are forever bombarded by myriad sources of information. Undoubtedly, this massive influx of information has been made possible by the coming of the "Information Age." Technology is constantly improving thereby impacting and changing the medium in which we receive our information. For example, the Internet provides individuals/personal investors with yet another manner personal and real estate-type information almost instantaneously. The explosion of information has left the personal investors to beg the question, where to begin and what types of information to process before making a decision?

This book on *Decision Making for Personal Investments: Real Estate Financing, Foreclosures and Other Issues* seeks to:

1. Introduce the individual investor to *six dominant pathways* for personal and real estate financial decisions.
2. Assist the individual investor in developing a conceptual *process thinking* framework upon which to base decisions on personal and real estate financial stewardship.
3. Assist the individual investor to achieve a working knowledge of techniques for evaluating financial data, for purposes of personal and real estate decision making.

Acknowledgments

This book owes a great debt to those researchers whose efforts laid the groundwork of areas in accounting, economics, finance, and psychology. We are thankful for the encouragement, suggestions, and counsel provided by many instructors, professionals, and students in writing this book. In addition, the contributions from other institutions and resources have aided in the production of this book. Our own research efforts have naturally fueled how we think about many of the aforementioned topics. Finally, last but not least, we would like to thank our family and friends, without their support this book would not have been possible.

Contents

List of Figures

List of Tables

CHAPTER 1

Six Dominant Pathways for Personal and Real Estate Decisions

Abstract This chapter presents a process thinking model that is an ideal adaptable structure that sheds light on critical pathways for decision-making purposes and eradicates rival alternative tentative assumptions. It integrates perception, information, judgment, and decision choice in order to reach resolution, settlement, or finding.

Keywords Process thinking model · Perception · Information · Judgment and decision choice

This book discusses a process thinking model in order to determine personal investing and real estate assessment of individuals (1) understanding the types of goals that can be reasonably accomplished in the situation, (2) increasing the salience of information that are important within the context of the situation, (3) forming expectations which can serve as a check on the accuracy of the situation assessment, and (4) identifying the typical actions to take.

We are likely to spend a great deal of time on making a decision based on how we feel or perceive a situation before we have assembled any information that will help us to make a calculated choice. Or we may base our decision choices based on what our mentors have done or what we think we are supposed to do. These are a small number of ways we make decision choices, which can prove to be costly or profitable.

W. Rodgers, T.G. McFarlin, *Decision Making for Personal Investment*,
DOI 10.1007/978-3-319-47849-4_1

The most significant point to remember is, there is no one certain technique to make a decision choice. It should all be based on your desired destination and you ought to seek out as much information as possible. The more we learn about the various segments of decision-making framework, the simpler it will be to make decision choices that will be the most beneficial.

The approaches we use to make decision choices will vary from time to time and some are least likely to get you where you want to be than others. For instance, when you use perceptual biases in making your decision choice you are diminishing your chances and choosing to let the outcome to be removed from control. It doesn't allow you to educate yourself on the outcome and is not an appropriate manner of making a decision choice due to the lack of effort exerted.

Another way we make decision choices is through pathways. We continue to make decision choices the way we always have. The way we were taught by our parents and/or through habit. This tactic only leads us in a circle and keeps us from ever-pursuing change or advancement. Finally, there are the six dominant pathways we have available to make decision choices. This is where we weigh our options, view the pros and cons and make sure that we are going to get our preferred result. This is the way we want to train our minds to make decision choices. It is an educated approach that permits us to practically determine the outcome. Smart decision making is all about perceptual expertise and making good judgments.

If ever you are at a point of not knowing why you are about to make a decision choice be sure to take a minute to stop and evaluate it. Analyze the type of decision it is and then choose to logically make the decision by assessing the pros and cons and selecting the answer that gives you long-term success. This should open up some thought and keep you from feeling the effects that will come if you simply choose to emotionally decide.

For some of the clever decision-making processes may cause feelings of anxiety or uncertainty. Due to the old conditioning and poor decision choice biases or heuristics (i.e., rule of thumb) that we are used to taking, a step onto new territory may seem intimidating and may cause some concern.

Moreover, the more personal the decision choice, the more difficult it may become to make a wise decision over one that will bring some kind of instantaneous happiness. In these types of situations we tend to slip out of objective thinking which keeps us from thinking clearly. Therefore, let's review the four cornerstones of decision making.

Four major concepts that affect personal and real estate financial decisions are:

Perception (P) ~ experiences, training and education
Information (I) ~ all available financial and non-financial information sources
Judgment (J) ~ the analysis of both perceptual processes and information sources
Decision choices (D) ~ involves selection of the best alternative solution or course of action

Decision making in this model is defined as a multi-stage, information-processing function in which cognitive processes are used to generate a set of outcomes. There have been differences of opinion about how many stages and subroutines within the phases exist and the order in which the stages occur. However, the three stages in the proposed model appear with some consistency in everyday life.

The model is presented in Fig. 1.1. Arrows from one concept to another indicate the assumed causal relationships that can be specified a priori using a decision-making approach. This model has been tested in various contexts including accounting, finance, auditing, military, and business ethics.

The main aspect of the process thinking modeling approach is that knowledge inputs are necessarily embedded in a context representing cognitive, behavioral, individual, and social that constrains their discovery and their usefulness in different problems. This aspect is described as "perception" in Fig. 1.1.

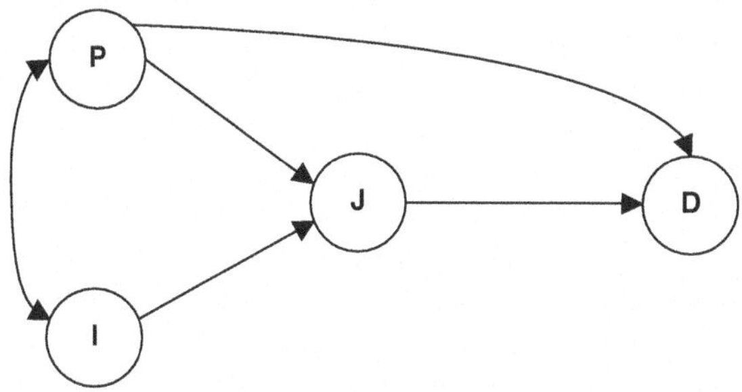

Where **P** = perception, **I** = information, **J** = judgment, and **D** = decision choice

Fig. 1.1 Process thinking model (Rodgers 2006)

In the first stage, since individuals typically process information subjectively, it is interdependent with perception in the conceptual model. Additionally, in this first stage, perception and information directly affect judgment. Normally, before individuals can make a decision choice, they encode the information and develop a representation for the problem.

In the second stage, perception and judgment can impact on decision choice. Perception-like heuristics and more deliberate strategies (judgment) are included in most decision choices.

The four concepts of "perception," "information," "judgment," and "decision choice" combine in different ways to make available for individual investors with six pathways to successful decision making. The six different pathways that investors attempt to implement in order to reach a financial decision are (Rodgers 2006) the following:

1. The expedient pathway
2. The ruling guide pathway
3. The analytical pathway
4. The revisionist pathway
5. The value-driven pathway
6. The global perspective pathway

The ***first pathway*** is **P→D**, the expedient pathway, which typically occurs in situations where a decision choice ought to be made rapidly. The ***second pathway*** is the **P→J→D**, the ruling guide pathway, whereby time pressures may be imperative but are not as immediate as the **P→D** pathway. For the **P→J→D** pathway, an investor frames the problem, analyzes it, and then makes a decision choice. The ***third pathway*** is **I→J→D**, designated as the analytical pathway whereby relevant and reliable information is the assurance of good decision choices. When utilizing this pathway, information will directly influence the judgment stage before a decision is made. Preferably, the information is predetermined and is weighted by other sources, without biases. The ***fourth pathway*** is **I→P→D**, the revisionist pathway by means of which information can influence the manner in that an individual investor perceptually frames the problem or situation before coming to a final decision. The information affects the perceptual frame greatly while one is aiming for a decision choice. In addition, information is considered an important piece of this decision-making process. The ***fifth pathway*** is **P→I→J→D**, or the value-driven pathway illustrates perceptual framing influence on information sources that impacts on judgment before a decision is made. The perceptual frame can change the information sources used to be analyzed in the judgment stage. Further, an individual's education, training, economic, and social perspective has a major influence on how a situation is handled. The ***sixth pathway*** is **I→P→J→D**, or the global perspective pathway clarifies how information reinforces investors to adjust their perceptions before the judgment (analysis) stage begins. Furthermore, this pathway provides that an open-minded decision choice is more likely to be made due to new information that has been received by an investor (Rodgers 2006).

Task characteristics of personal investing such as investment type (bond, stock, real estate), time period, dividend or interest returns, etc., suggest seeking either patterns or functional relations in a situation. Pattern seeking is induced if the situation provides information that is highly organized (e.g., tables and charts of investment performance) and if individuals are required to produce coherent explanations of their investments. Functional relation seeking is induced if the information is not organized in a coherent manner and if the person is required to provide descriptions or predictions. Application of individuals' perceptions to external information can create a likelihood of mistakes, resulting in heuristics and biases (discussed below) of the perceptual system and/or a mismatch to the external information. The closer the match the more relevant is the coherence between perception and information. If the coherence between the two concepts is weak, then one of the following possible scenarios may exist:

1. An individual investor's framing of the problem may conflict with the external information;
2. The information may be providing confusing signals that cannot be properly matched with their perception;
3. The personal investor does not understand the external information; and
4. The personal investor may not trust the quality of the information.

The expertise of investors can influence how a particular problem is perceptually framed. Experts are known to strategize and encode knowledge differently from those without the same expertise level. As personal investors' knowledge increases, their ability to gather information, to recognize a familiar pattern, and to attend to critical indicators while ignoring less important features becomes more and more enhanced over time. In an investment environment, an effective investor is distinguished by an ability to frame the problem well. Further, individuals' behaviors can be classified as skill based, rule based, and knowledge based. *Skill-based investment behavior* comprises sensorimotor performance (e.g., talking, automobile driving), which functions smoothly and efficiently without conscious attention. *Rule-based investment behavior* is shaped by rules and know-how that can be stated plainly by the individual investors. *Knowledge-based investment behavior* is effective action in unique situations, which compels a profound understanding of the nature of the situation and explicit consideration of objectives and options. The misuse or lack of use of a certain investment behavior may result in bias behavior. That is, strategies employed by individual investors are fashioned by such environmental elements as task complexity and time pressures. The following are tips/advices on how to prevent irrational/biased personal investment decisions:

a. inclination to assign undue weight to the first evidence attained,
b. overconfidence on information that have taken on extreme values,
c. propensity to seek evidence that confirms the current premise (i.e., confirmation bias),
d. propensity to reason about only one or two hypotheses at a time (i.e., belief bias),
e. propensity to be overconfident (illusory of control),
f. aspiration to maintain consistency even if that means devaluing or ignoring important,
g. confidence in illusory correlations,
h. overly conservative expectations, and
i. constructing conclusions on hindsight (i.e., "I knew it all along" or hindsight bias).

By the same token, on biases in probabilistic reasoning includes:

a. to be unduly persuaded by the cognitive availability of information, and to misconstrue this characteristic for frequency;
b. to anchor judgments on initial estimates;
c. to access the likelihood of an event based on familiarity or stereotyping rather than objective frequency; and
d. to overestimate the frequency of rare events.

In Fig. 1.1, *perception* and *information* may influence judgment. A personal investor's framing or formulation (i.e., perception) of the problem can directly influence the structuring of the analysis (i.e., judgment) stage. Structuring can take several forms. For example, whether a decision maker chooses to use compensatory, non-compensatory or both methods rests heavily upon how the situation is designed for use.

Compensatory decision making encompasses classifying a set of elements pertinent to the decision choice, allocating a relative significance or weight to each element, calculating an overall score for each option centered on the element weight, and selecting the option with the best score. Compensatory decision making is based on utility maximization since the option(s) with the highest sum of the weighted utilities are selected. In compensatory decisions, a negative value on one element can be compensated by an equal or higher value on another element. For example, an expensive airline ticket (negative attribute) for one airline may be compensated by the better frequent flyer program (positive attribute) of that airline.

In contrast, non-compensatory decision making are those that make simpler the compensatory process by employing heuristics to promptly evaluate the alternatives with little effort. Non-compensatory decision making can provide quicker decision choices with satisfactory losses of accuracy. For example, in a non-compensatory strategy, an expensive airline ticket eliminates that option from the consideration set, with the better frequent flyer program unable to compensate for the expensive airline ticket feature.

The model presented in Fig. 1.1 allows personal investors to adaptively choose pathways in response to different task demands and that may require non-compensatory heuristics that allow for prompt decision choices. The process thinking viewpoint in Fig. 1.1 suggests that the traditional compensatory view of utility maximization and rational decision making may not be sufficient for certain tasks due to uncertainty, time pressures, ill-structured information, and changing environments.

Therefore, an individual investor ought to know an adequate set of different pathways to make selections. Difficulty will result if a needed pathway is not known or if an incorrect pathway is implemented for a problem. Investors should use selective knowledge that enables them to select pathways forming a useful solution.

This book advances that knowledge is embedded in "*judgment*" in our model (Fig. 1.1). Further, this knowledge represents procedural knowledge.

Procedural knowledge represents knowledge about how to perform a task. Procedural knowledge can be viewed as in terms of if-then condition-action rules, which stipulate that if a particular condition occurs, therefore a particular action takes place. Finally, procedural knowledge is acquired through task experience.

The transferal of knowledge between declaration knowledge (refers to unchanging, factual information) and procedural knowledge is an interactive process, which feeds upon itself constantly. The result of this process is viewed as a skill acquisition acquired by individual investors. Further, skill acquisition or ability enables investors to refine their operational skills, which influence their decision choices. For example, investors are known to use two strategies consisting of "decomposition" and "conversion." Decomposition permits investors to reduce a problem into subsets by drawing on their existing knowledge to make inferences, add constraints, and determine a small set of variables. This process enables the problem to be "converted" into one, which may be solved by postulating actions addressing the perceived causes. Skill acquisition can be viewed as a multifaceted process that includes knowledge and information acquisition, as well as the effects of perceptual processes.

From the *information* set, individual investors seek to identify important attributes or properties. Investors attempt to size down from the available information to a more manageable set. This information set is selected from the external environment, and properly coded, and becomes part of the knowledge structures. Knowledge structures comprise of declarative knowledge, which is transformed into procedural knowledge. It is the procedural knowledge that converts skill operations into the judgment (analysis) stage.

Perception can directly impact upon decision choice. Time pressures, vague goals, and high stakes may not provide an investor with the luxury of going through an exhaustive analysis. In these types of circumstances, an investor's pattern recognition and ability to formulate a strategy may provide a more realistic response in a dynamic environment. They may rely on their abilities to recognize and aptly classify a situation. When a situation is recognized, investors implement their experience in terms of formulating expectancies, plausible goals, relevant cues, and typical actions. Implementation may follow due to time pressures and ambiguity. Likewise, familiarity with certain tasks may provide investors with the ability to use heuristics adapted to the problem at hand. Finally, investors may decompose a problem into several parts, whereby some parts of their analysis will not require a detail analysis through the judgment stage.

Summary

In conclusion, the *process thinking model* is an ideal adaptable structure that sheds light on critical pathways for decision-making purposes and eradicates rival alternative tentative assumptions. It integrates perception, information, judgment, and decision choice in order to reach resolution, settlement, or finding. This approach also considers external conditions such as changing environments, time pressures, incomplete information, and levels of expertise in order to make successful investment decisions.

Reference

Rodgers, W. 2006. *Process Thinking: Six Pathways to Successful Decision Making.* New York: IUniverse.

CHAPTER 2

Understanding the Decision-Making Process for Personal Investments

Abstract Contingent upon the circumstances, "six dominant pathways" are part of, or all of, the major forms of decision making, that is perception, information, judgment, and decision choice. These circumstances entail the degree of an individual's expertise, completeness of information sources, stableness of the environment, and time pressures.

Keywords Decision making · Expertise · Complete information · Stable environment · Time pressures

People are faced with investment decisions all the time, even though most of the time they are not aware of it. Should they open a stock trading account to capture market movement, or just invest in a long-term bond to gain stable yield? Should they purchase or lease a car or a house? These choices will have different financial impact. What is more, some investments are not simply in the form of finances; we also decide whether to invest in our human capital by receiving further education. Unlike in the 1960s when "investing" was something only wealthy people did, today millions of middle-income Americans hold a substantial portion of their savings in mutual funds and are interested in knowing how to best allocate it across asset classes. As we move further into the twenty-first century, investment decisions of individuals are a matter of great consideration among business analysts, public officials, and ordinary people worldwide.

W. Rodgers, T.G. McFarlin, *Decision Making for Personal Investment*,
DOI 10.1007/978-3-319-47849-4_2

Since people invest on a regular basis and there is more disposable income now than ever before, this book is designed to assist investors in making sound personal investment decisions and present them with options available to recover from bad decisions they may have already made. We will do this by (1) exploring the individual investor's decision-making process when faced with investment choices, (2) examining the bad real estate investment decisions millions of Americans made over the last decade that led to the housing bubble in 2006 and the credit crisis in 2008, and (3) providing examples to show how some investors have overcome bad decisions.

Generally Accepted Investment Principles

Business strategists, through extensive research and experiment, have generally agreed on a set of practical guidelines that are called generally accepted investment principles. These principles are summarized in the following manner. First, investors should have an emergency fund invested in short-term safe assets. This fund should be held outside a retirement account to avoid the tax and other penalties generally associated with having to withdraw funds prematurely from a retirement account. Second, funds saved for retirement should be invested primarily in equities and long-term fixed-income securities. Third, as the investor's age advances, the fraction of assets invested in equities should decline. A popular rule of thumb regarding the age-equity relationship is that the percentage of one's portfolio to invest in equities should be 100 minus one's age. Therefore, a person of 30 years old should invest 70 % in equities, and a person aged 70 should invest 30 % in equities.[1]

Fourth, the fraction of assets invested in equities increases with wealth because a wealthier individual should be able to handle more risk. Fifth, tax-advantaged assets, such as municipal bonds, should be held outside one's retirement account, and only investors in high tax brackets should invest in them. More generally, assets that are taxed more heavily (such as taxable bonds) should be held in a retirement account and those that are taxed less heavily (such as non-dividend-paying equities) could be held outside a retirement account. Sixth, all investors should diversify their total portfolios across asset classes, and the equity portion should be well diversified across industries and companies.

While the guidelines above are generally accepted on average, we also have to acknowledge the fact that the optimal investment mix for any particular individual or household may deviate from the general principles because investment is a personalized endeavor. Thus, special circumstances and risk preferences will differ considerably across investors. For example, married couples who both work may be able to invest a larger portion of their wealth in equities than a married couple with a single income. Furthermore, people with uncertain job prospects may want to invest less in equities than people with relatively predictable income.

Financial Goals and Investment Category

Today, numerous investments are available for potential investors. However, although we recognize that people act upon general practiced investment principles, we emphasize the importance of the different goals of personal investment. In turn, the type of investment an individual chooses reflects their financial goals. In order to discuss our six decision processes in greater detail, we have categorized people's investment goals into three classes: maximizing return, minimizing risk, and personal necessities.

1. *Maximizing return.* Many people focus their financial goals on increasing their return on investment (ROI). The pursuit of personal ROI is to gain the most financially from their investment. For some investors, this means getting the highest financial return regardless of any nonmonetary impact on the investor himself or on the society. For some other investors, the return is more inclusive; besides personal ROI, they consider the impact the investment will have on the environment as a whole. Historically speaking, equities are the type of investment that yields the highest return overall. In fact, large stocks have on average generated close to 10 % of annual return since the end of the Second World War. Therefore, in our discussion of maximizing return, we refer to investment in the equities market.
2. *Minimizing risk.* A large amount of investors are risk-averse. For these types of investors, they expect to get a slightly higher return than putting money in a money market account. This is mainly to guard against future inflation. The major concern of this group of investors is to keep its risk of exposure to a minimum; theses investors are willing to accept a low ROI if it provides safer financial assets. Typical investments of choice are government treasury bonds,

municipal bonds, and certain tax-favored assets. Purchase of CD accounts is also a choice investment. These are all in the form of long-term fixed-income securities. Thus, in later discussions on minimizing risks, we will focus on different types of fixed-income securities.

3. *Personal necessities.* Aside from maximizing return and minimizing risk, some financial goals are based on personal necessities, such as the need to purchase a house or a car, or to pursue higher education. These are highly personalized investment decisions; since the goal is to fulfill an individual need, the investor will put less emphasis on personal ROI and more focus on the consequence of the investment. Therefore, decisions made based on personal necessities are typically taking out a mortgage on a house or a loan on an automobile.

Decision Process Models

Decision models we implement in this book are models from the book *Process Thinking: Six Pathways to Successful Decision Making* by Professor Waymond Rodgers. Four major factors are used to develop six decision processes. The four factors are *perception (P)*, *information (I)*, *judgment (J)*, and *decision choice (D)*. These four concepts combine in different ways to provide investors with six pathways to successful decision making. The six different pathways that investors use to reach a financial decision are the following:

1. The expedient pathway
2. The ruling guide pathway
3. The analytical pathway
4. The revisionist pathway
5. The value-driven pathway
6. The global perspective pathway

Selection of a particular pathway can hedge upon circumstances that entail the extent of one's expertise, completeness of information sources, stableness of the environment, and time pressures. Expertise represents the knowledge or skill level that a person possesses in solving a problem or completing a task. Stable environment represents consistently repeating activities that enable us to use the previous patterns to help anticipate future events. Incomplete information, inadequate understanding and/or undifferentiated alternatives may render information to be limited or unreliable in contributing to a decision choice. Finally, time pressures may prevent a thorough analysis by the use of the judgment stage.

In the following chapter, we will discuss these six pathways in detail with examples for different financial goals. By analyzing different decision processes and different financial goals, we hope to uncover certain successful decision-making processes in the area of personal investment.

Summary

In conclusion, contingent upon the circumstances, the six dominant pathways will use part or all of the major forms of decision making, that is perception, information, judgment and decision choice. These circumstances entail the degree of an individual's expertise, completeness of information sources, stableness of the environment, and time pressures. Moreover, the combinations of the dominant six pathways illustrate how forming our decision-making processes into a network can influence the choices in personal investments that we make.

Note

1. This general rule of thumb does not apply to all situations. Later discussions on specific decision pathways will cover this investment in greater detail.

CHAPTER 3

Six Decision Pathways for Personal Investment Decision Making

Abstract These six pathways representing *the expedient pathway, the ruling guide pathway, the analytical pathway, the revisionist pathway, the value-driven pathway, and the global perspective pathway* are one way to relating maximizing returns, minimizing risk, and understanding personal necessities to making decisions.

Keywords Expedient pathway · Ruling guide pathway · Analytical pathway · Revisionist pathway · Value-driven pathway · Global perspective pathway

This chapter centers on six dominant decision-making pathways described as follows: *the expedient pathway, the ruling guide pathway, the analytical pathway, the revisionist pathway, the value-driven pathway, and the global perspective pathway*. These six dominant decision-making pathways are instrumental for individual investors to relate maximizing returns, minimizing risk, and understanding personal necessities when making decision choices.

1. **The expedient pathway P→D**
2. **The ruling guide pathway P→J→D**
3. **The analytical pathway I→J→D**
4. **The revisionist pathway I→P→D**

W. Rodgers, T.G. McFarlin, *Decision Making for Personal Investment*,
DOI 10.1007/978-3-319-47849-4_3

5. **The value-driven pathway P→I→J→D**
6. **The global perspective pathway I→P→J→D**

Expedient Pathway

As our first decision pathway's name suggests, it is the least time-consuming way to reach a decision choice. The missing component of information here indicates that the decision maker does not have to depend on reliable and relevant information to make a decision. The decision maker gives great attention to the "P" or perception. Perception serves to frame their environment: prior education, cultural background, and personal emotions will all influence the final decision. They retrieve from memory what is deemed to be important and make a decision based on what they believe is true. In this "shortcut" decision-making pathway, little consideration is given to available information and a great deal of consideration is given to how the world is personally perceived. The thinking process is represented in Fig. 3.1.

The lack of information in the expedient thinking process has both advantages and disadvantages. This decision pathway has a significant advantage over other pathways because it is useful under intense time pressure. Professionals, such as police officers and emergency room doctors, who deal with life-threatening situations, have to make decisions within a fraction of a second. For example, police officers and emergency room doctors cannot afford to sort through all relevant and reliable information before deciding to apprehend a suspect or operate on the injured;

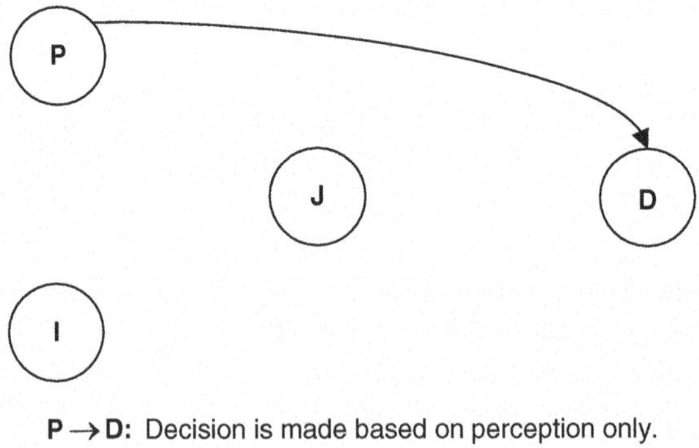

Fig. 3.1 Expedient pathway decision-making process

otherwise, they could potentially put more lives in danger. They must rely on their experience or expertise to make a quick decision. Although, most of us do not deal with critical decisions on a daily basis, we still use the expedient pathway in our daily lives. When information is unavailable, or we do not need precise information, we are more likely to use perception alone to lead to a decision. Fifty percent of the time, at most, can information be deemed useful for decision-making purposes (Rodgers 2006). For this reason, the expedient thinking process is the most widely used decision-making process today.

Obviously, expedient thinking poses great risks, too. Since all decisions are made solely based on personal perception, personal biases occur when a person is making their final decision. Many scandals involving management fraud stem from this type of decision process. If the management team wants to receive a higher bonus, they will manipulate their financial statements to show a better performance. They do not take into consideration the company policy, industry guidelines, or even legal consequences. They base the decision solely on their personal desire to earn more money.

As a result, although we save valuable time when using the **P→D** pathway, we also risk making a costly decision. Next, we will look at how the expedient decision-making process works in the realm of personal investment.

Maximizing Return

As discussed in the first section of this book, people have different goals in their investment decisions. Maximizing returns appears to be a common goal. When we have fulfilled all our living and entertainment needs and still have capital left in our bank account (if only this is true!), we will want this excess cash to generate a sizable return. Many people choose to invest in the stock market, since stocks generally yield a higher average annual return than bonds and mutual funds. In fact, large stocks have on average generated close to 10 % of annual return since the end of the Second World War. Further, in the last 30 years, the higher percentage of the holding on stocks, the greater the average returns to the investor.

Hence, if the investors' goal is to maximize return on their investment, they will most likely go ahead and put their money in the stock market because they have identified that stocks yield the highest return. Thus, the expedient pathway becomes a dominant thinking process when the decision maker's goal is to maximize return. The investors will most likely ignore the information that, even though stocks yield higher returns, they also have the highest risk. Yet, in the **P→D** pathway, information does not come into play; the investors will base their decision solely on the perception that they will earn the highest return possible by investing all their capital in the stock market.

Minimizing Risk

If an investor's financial goal is to simply safeguard his capital against inflation, that is, preserving the purchasing power of their cash without incurring any risk, the investor will mostly likely engage in investment activities that minimize all risks. Government treasury bonds are usually the preferred choice. Since a country's government poses the least risk of non-repayment, an expedient decision maker who seeks to minimize risk will use this judgment to invest in government treasury bills. Again, since information is lacking in this **P→D** pathway, the investor will not take into account that governments, stable as they are, still have default risks. For example, the Eurozone debt crisis has shown that governments, Greece, in particular, can also be risky investment targets. Hence, we can take note that the Greek government bond has been decreased to the point that it is almost a junk bond. Accordingly, this is due to the fact that Greek government debt was 170 % of the country's current GDP. Investors have lost confidence in Greek bonds; additionally, there is widespread belief that Greece will default on these government bonds. Although government bonds generally have less risk than other types of bonds, it is still possible that certain governments cannot repay their debt. If the investors do not consider this relevant information, as is the case with the expedient decision maker, they will lose a significant amount of their investments if the government defaults on the bond.

Personal Necessity

Another goal of people's investments comes out of personal necessity. As indicated in the first section, we also invest in a house, car, education, or retirement. These investments come from our need to better our lives and careers. When we want to purchase a house, this desire will lead one to enter into a loan even though it is much more costly than the average market rates. Since information is unavailable, or we choose not to rely on information, our only purpose is to fulfill our personal need. As a result, the expedient thinking process becomes the dominant pathway in such a situation. We will buy the house, the car, or the most impressive refrigerator no matter how high the interest rate is. This is exactly why millions of people are burdened with high mortgage, car, and credit card payments today; they did not refer to the information regarding their interest rate when they made the purchase. They perceived the merchandise to be desirable, and they signed the loan documents or slid their card to fulfill that desire.

As we have seen, the expedient thinking process is the most convenient way to make a decision. It is probably the most common decision pathway that people are using today, although many are unaware of the process. In certain critical situations, this **P→D** pathway serves us well. However, in the area of personal investment, when we are not faced with time constraints, the expedient pathway is not the best process when trying to make the best financial decision. No matter what our financial goal is, we always have to take risk into consideration: high return brings high risk, low return will not eliminate risk, and personal necessity disguises risk. Without the help of reliable and relevant information on risks, investors will more than likely end up making bad financial decisions.

The Ruling Guide Pathway

This pathway is generally used in situations in which people have no time pressure to make decisions (Rodgers 2006). The missing or unclear information will cause decision makers to rely on their internal or external rules, rather than on any reliable or relevant information to make decisions. In other words, they make decisions on the linkage of perception through judgment. The previous experiences of the decision makers formed an embedded procedure set to do analysis and make decisions. The decision made may have pleasant or unpleasant results since sometimes the environment may be changing or unstructured in which the rules may not apply. The thinking process is represented below in Fig. 3.2.

As shown in Fig. 3.2, people make decisions based on their judgment that is linked to their perception. Like the expedient pathway, information is also missing in this pathway. This pathway also has its advantages and disadvantages. Similar to the expedient pathway, the ruling guide pathway is less time-consuming. In a stable environment, people who utilize this path can quickly make decisions based on their embedded rules that formed through their previous experience or education or believes. However, since the environment is changing, the rules sometimes may not be suitable for the

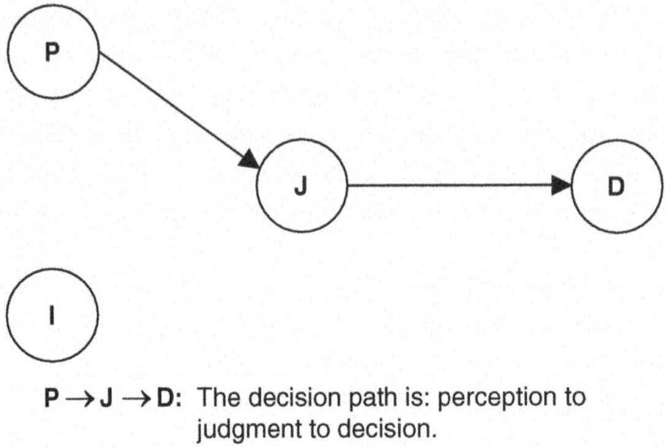

Fig. 3.2 The ruling guide pathway

new situation and the decision made based on the internal or external rules may cause unpleasant results. Therefore, ignoring information will bring high level of risk. In the area of personal investment, when the investing environment is stable and every stakeholder and company follow the rules, utilizing the ruling guide pathway will be more efficient and effective. However, in a changing environment, the **P→J→D** pathway may lead to wrong financial decisions.

Maximizing Return

With the goal to maximize return, under the **P→J→D** pathway, as we discussed in Fig. 3.2, investors may still choose to invest in the stock market with the perception that the stock will bring the highest return. Unlike under the **P→D** pathway, the investors have no time pressure and are more likely to follow the embedded rules or procedures that are linked to their personal perception to make decisions. When the environment is stable, this pathway is more efficient and effective. However, the judgment that is linked to his/her perception may not be able to apply to the changing environment. If no information is taken into account, unexpected loss may occur. Let's take the stock market for example. The rules tell us that every company will file their 10 K accurately without any fraud information (**P**). Therefore, the investors can look at a company's financial statement to do ratio analysis to evaluate the value of the company's stock and get the amount of return (**J**). After this process, they can make their decision (**D**).

This ruling guide thinking process will help decision makers make decision efficiently and effectively. However, ignoring additional information may cause problems. Take Enron for example. Enron manipulated its financial reports to mislead the investors and caused lots of loss. If the investors did not pay attention to Enron's activities, news reports, and other related information but only followed the investing rules that all the financial statements filed by the companies were trustful, they would have suffered great losses. Let's also take Lehman Brother's stock investment for example. The investors normally invest in the stocks that have good credit ratings. If the stock credit rating is high, they should invest money in this stock and expect higher return; if the stock credit rating is low, they should not invest their money in this stock, since they believe that the credit rating agencies are trustworthy based on their many years of experiences and education. For example, when examining a particular company's S&P credit rating scores over time a few things come to mind. First, when the rating is higher, the investor will invest in the stock; when the rating declines, the investor will withdraw money to prevent loss. Through this pathway, they can realize the goal of maximum return. However, sometimes, the credit rating agencies are not trustful. They may give misleading information to investors due to various conflicts of interest. Therefore, investors need to analyze additional information to evaluate the credit rating agencies and evaluate the company to make wise decision choices.

Therefore, when everything is stable, the ruling guide thinking process can make the investing decision making more efficient and effective. However, when the environment is changing, without the help of information, investors can easily make financial decision choices that lead to high risk and huge loss.

Minimizing Risk

With the goal to minimize risk and safeguard investors' asset, under the **P→J→D** pathway, people may make a decision to put their money in a "risk free" investment, such as certificate of deposits (CDs), which are considered the safest investment among different investing vehicles, including corporate bonds and stocks since Federal Deposit Insurance Corporation (FDIC) protects most of the CD's accounts (**P**). Following this rule, the investors can evaluate the risk between CDs, corporate bonds, and stocks (**J**) and choose CDs to minimize risk (**D**). However, additional information such as an increasing inflation rate will cause the

CD risk again. The high inflation rate will cause the real interest rate to be negative and, therefore, make investors' money worthless.

During the period of time from 1900 to 1970, the inflation rate is very stable. However, since 1970–2012, it increases dramatically. Inflation is one of the biggest risk factors to the conservative investors. If investors only follow the rules believing that a CD is totally risk free, they will also suffer loss because of the time value of money. Nonetheless, this story tells us the power of investors' money may decline year by year. Jeremy Walter calculated that the value of one dollar has declined 86 % over the last 47 years, which means it takes $7 now to buy what cost $1 in 1965 (Walter 2012). Therefore, the money they invested today will be worth less in the future. Consequently, additional information needs to be considered when investors make an investing evaluation. The rules may be changed in a changing or unstructured environment.

Personal Necessity

As the goal of personal necessity, in a person's life span, people normally follow the rules that are embedded in their thinking habit. In the early stage of life, under the ruling guide pathway, investors will invest the money into education since it will give them good opportunities to get a job to support themselves. In the middle stage of life, they will get married, have kids, and invest money into a house, cars, kids' education, and retirement accounts. In the old stage of the life, investors may get the money from their retirement accounts and then invest the money into travel, entertainment, or supporting kids to get a better education. In a stable economic and political environment, this pathway dominates the decision-making process throughout a person's entire life. It is efficient and effective. Most people follow their internal or external rules that form along with their experiences, education, and beliefs. However, when the environment is changing, this pathway may not be effective. Take the real estate area, for example. In California, especially Northern California, the average home price is extremely high. If investors grow up in mid America, say, Dallas, Texas, then move to Northern California for college, graduate, and find good jobs there, following their internal rules, they may consider investing money in a house in Northern California since they have had a stable life there. However, unlike Dallas, the house prices in Northern California are significantly higher since a lot of wealthy foreigners invest money into California real estate market, which causes high housing prices. Although housing price is declining in most areas of America, housing price in Northern California remains firm. Furthermore, the salaries the investors get from their jobs are too low to afford a house. At the same time, the interest rate on loans is very high in Northern California. If investors invest money in the real estate market, they will most likely not be able to afford to pay off the debt, as well as save money for their children's education and even their retirement plans. In this scenario, investors need to change to adapt to the environment. They may consider relocating to Dallas to have a better life there.[1]

In summary, we have seen the advantage and disadvantage of applying the *ruling guide pathway* in the investment decision-making process. When the environment is stable, this pathway will help investors reach a decision more favorable and the process will be more efficient. However, when the environment is changing, the rules may not apply. Without evaluating relevant and relative information, the investors may face unpleasant results.

The Analytical Pathway

The analytical pathway incorporates the use of relevant and reliable information for our decision-making process. The major difference that sets this pathway apart from the previous two pathways is the importance of information. Whereas perceptual framing influences judgment and decision choices in both the expedient and ruling guide pathways, it is not to be found in the analytical pathway. As the name suggests, this pathway involves a great deal of analysis of the available information and its impact on judgment.

As indicated in Fig. 3.3, the typical decision-making process for the analytical pathway includes "specifying the problem, identifying all factors, weighting factors, identifying all alternatives, rating alternatives on each factor, and choosing the optimal alternative" (Rodgers 2006). The advantage of using this pathway is, of course, accuracy; information is reliable and relevant and personal preference will not influence our judgment. We only make a decision based on the analysis of precise and complete information; therefore, the choice we make is the most useful alternative. However, since information is rarely complete and the environment is constantly changing, if we cannot ensure we have relevant and reliable information to begin with, the use of **I→J→D** will lead to an ill-informed, useless decision. In the area of personal investment, good

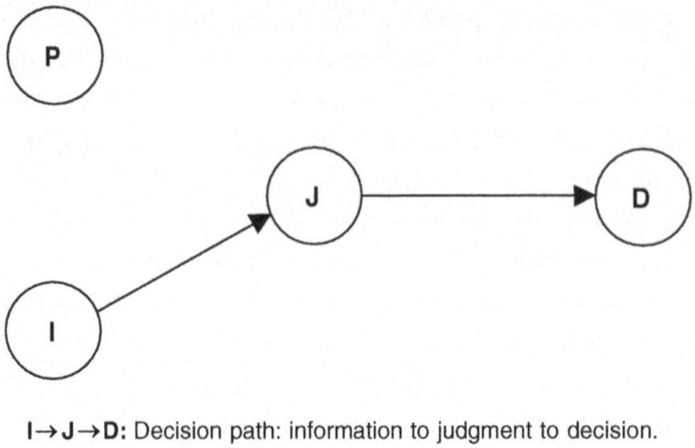

Fig. 3.3 The analytical pathway

financing decisions utilizing all relevant data will lead to large returns; bad financing decisions using unreliable data will, of course, make the investor end up in dire situations.

Maximizing Return

As we have shown in earlier sections, investors who look to maximize their return will more likely consider investing in the stock market. Since high return brings high risk, lack of proper evaluation of potential risks will make investing in the stock market undesirable. With the analytical pathway, we put great emphasis on information. When we need to choose which stock or a portfolio of stocks to invest in, we will resort to relevant and reliable information. Typically, an investor will look at the stock's past performances: the average return, standard deviation of the returns, dividend distribution policy, the company's financial statements, and financial analysts' projections on future earnings. After the investors have gathered this information, they will weigh this information and conduct some evaluation of their own. Plenty of stock price evaluation models are at the investor's disposal: financial ratio analysis, capital asset pricing model, dividend discount model, Black-Scholes option pricing model, etc. These are all proven to be useful tools for stock evaluation; the analytical investor will then weigh potential risks against potential return and form his or her own judgment on the stocks. Finally, they will decide whether to invest in that particular stock or portfolio of stocks.

Compared with the previous two pathways, the analytical pathway is grounded on available information and investors have a better chance of making sound investing decision on stocks when using it. However, stock investment is investing in the future; stock prices today depend on speculations of future performance of the stock. We can gather all relevant and reliable information on past performance; we can also judge that the stock we choose has been performing well so far; but that is not enough to decide whether it is a good stock for future earnings.

Studies have shown that even with today's vast amount of information and evaluation tools available, investors are not earning high returns. Every year, Dalbar, a market-research firm, releases a study that compares investors' returns with the performance of the stock market. Standard Poor's 500-stock index returned 9.1 % annualized for the 20-year period through 2010, but Dalbar found that the average investor in stocks earned just 3.8 % a year (Frick 2011). Therefore, the analytical pathway is not necessarily going to yield an optimal stock investment decision because information on future performance, which is the heart of stock evaluation, is unavailable.

Minimizing Risk

We can clearly see from the calculation above that although the tax-exempt bond appears to have a lower before-tax return of 8 %, as opposed to the corporate fully taxable bond of 20 %, the after-tax premium of the tax-exempt bond is actually higher than the fully taxable corporate bond (Table 3.1). Without the help of relevant and reliable information, the risk-adverse investor may likely select a corporate bond due to limited information pertaining to "risk factors." The reason for rejection of the tax-exempt bond by an analytical-type thinker is that it has a lower before-tax required rate of return, which indicates a higher risk than the corporate

Table 3.1 Investors' rate of return between fully taxable and tax-exempt bonds

	Fully taxable bond (%)	*Tax-exempt bond (%)*
Required pretax return	20	8
Required pretax risk premium	7	3
Explicit tax rate	61.53	0
% of return taxable	100	0
After-tax risk premium	2.69	3

bond. In fact, after weighing all relevant information and conducting a valid calculation, the analytical decision maker may discover that the seemingly low risk-bearing tax-exempt municipal bond has a higher after-tax risk premium. Therefore, the optimal decision to minimize risk is to invest in the tax-exempt municipal bond.

The **I→J→D** pathway is useful when the investment goal is to minimize risk. Available information and evaluation tools will help investors look through misleading information and align correct information with their financial goal. This pathway has proven to be most useful in a stable environment (as indicated in the bond example) where information such as tax rate, required rate of return, and taxable portion on the bond is true. In the cases where this information is not available or cannot be fully trusted, we may need to resort to other decision pathways to decide on the investment.

To achieve the goal of safe investment, an investor is inclined to invest in government treasury bills because a nation will likely to have less default risk and a corporation. We have seen that even with governments, some have higher risks than are traditionally believed. Therefore, information and analysis on available information are critical when choosing a low risk bond investment. The analytical pathway will serve us well when trying to choose the least risky investment. Consider a situation in which the investor is faced with deciding between a fully taxable corporate bond and an interest-exempt municipal bond. Information available on the two bonds are given and calculated as follows.

Personal Necessity

When we have to fulfill a personal desire, such as owning a house or a car, the expedient and ruling guide pathways are likely to dominate since they are heavily influenced by personal preference. As such, decisions made are likely to be ill-informed and costly. With the analytical pathway, the investor will seek information and evaluate alternatives before deciding to purchase a car or a house. For example, if the investor deems owning a car is necessary, does he pay for the car right away or does he lease with the option to buy a few years later? When relying solely on perceptual framing, the investor may choose to buy right away to fulfill his needs with a high interest rate attached to the purchase agreement. An analytical decision maker will more likely look at the lease terms, evaluate them against the purchase terms, consider the useful life of the vehicle, and then make the most sensible decision. He may decide to lease first and buy later if he thinks the interest rate is unreasonably high so that leasing becomes less costly.

The same process of analysis occurs when purchasing a house, too. Typically a homeowner can choose to buy certain points when they take out a mortgage so that the interest rate will be lower. Ignoring information will make such a decision more like gambling; deciding whether to buy points or not and how many points to buy is at the mercy of luck. Yet an investor who is utilizing available information will feel more at ease: he will consider the mortgage payments before and after buying points, expected years he is going to live in the house, availability of cash to buy points, etc. After certain break-even analysis, he will confidently decline or accept the option of buying certain points to reduce mortgage interest. Therefore, the analytical process thinking pathway is highly useful in making financing decisions regarding personal necessities, too.

In summary, we have seen the advantages and disadvantages of applying the analytical pathway in the realm of personal decisions. When information, such as projections on future events, is incomplete this decision pathway is not going to be helpful for investors. Without relevant and reliable information, the pathway's heavy reliance on information is bound to yield undesirable outcome. When information can be determined, the decision based on analysis of useful information is going to benefit the investor a great deal. As the examples have shown, when the investor is not focusing on maximizing return, the analytical decision pathway is most useful in arriving at sound financial decisions.

Revisionist Pathway

The revisionist pathway implies that the available information sources (**I**) can influence the investors' framing (**P**) of the problem before arriving at a decision (**D**) (Rodgers 2006). Similar **to P→D,** the investors are in a situation that may have time pressure and therefore need to make a decision immediately. The major difference between the revisionist pathway and the expedient pathway is that the available information can affect the investors' perception and thereby change the investor's decisions that will be made under the **P→D** pathway. Figure 3.4 represents the thinking process of the revisionist pathway **(I→P→D)**.

As shown in Fig. 3.4, the judgment is missing in this pathway. Investors' perception will be influenced by the information before they

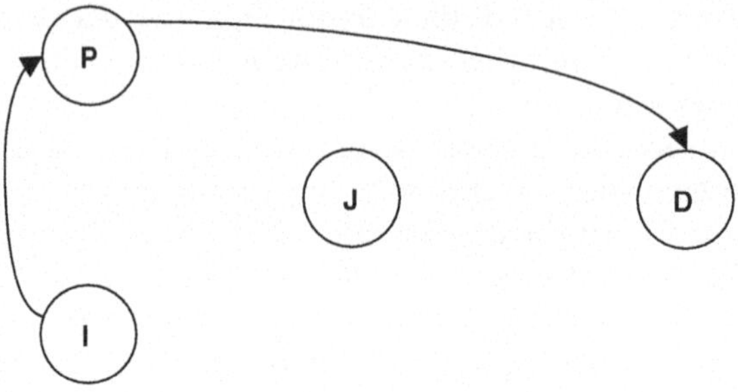

Fig. 3.4 The revisionist pathway

make a decision. This pathway also has its advantages and disadvantages. The relevant and useful information will help investors adjust their perception and make good decisions. If the information is consistent with the perception, the investor will have more confidence to make a decision. However, some information may be biased and noisy, which will influence the investor's perception and lead to the wrong decision.

Maximizing Return

As we discussed in the expedient pathway section, 100 % stocks investment generally yields a higher average annual return than bonds and mutual funds (Fig. 3.4). The rate is close to 10 %. Therefore, investors' perception is stock will give them highest return (**P**). However, as we discussed in the analytical pathway section, Robert Frick's "How to Be a Better Investor" delivered the information to us that although S&P 500 returned 9.1 % annualized for the 20-year period through 2010, the average investor in stocks earned just 3.8 % a year (**I**). If the investors get this information, their perception that the stocks will give around 10 % return will revise to 3.8 % and therefore, they will not invest 100 % in stock. Let's also take the IPO of Facebook for example. The investors may have the perception that the IPO of Facebook will be very successful and the stock price will increase dramatically based on their personal experience with Facebook. Therefore, if under the expedient pathway, the investor will go ahead and purchase the Facebook stock with the hope to get good return. However, if they read the analysts' articles in the *Wall Street Journal* about Facebook's stock possibly being overpriced, they would probably change their perception and decide not to purchase Facebook's stock right after its Initial Public Offering (IPO). For example, let's assume that the trends of Facebook's stock price in 5 days are declining. We can tell from this trend that the price of Facebook's stock may decline a lot (Shayni et al. 2012).

However, some information may be biased and mislead investors. Because of time pressure, the investor has no time to make an analysis. Therefore, the biased information will lead them to make a wrong decision. Let's look at another IT company, Google. The first day that Google went public, many analysts said it would not last long. Therefore, the investors that originally would purchase Google stock might stop purchasing since the analyzers argued that the Internet bubble would break. Therefore, the information provided by the analyzers was biased and did not bring accurate results. If the investors want to invest in a long term, full investigation of the information and then evaluation need to be taken into account (**J**).

Minimizing Risk

As we also discussed in regard to the analytical pathway, an investor is inclined to invest in government treasury bills because a nation will likely have less default risk than a corporation (**P**). Therefore, before the investors receive any information, they may make decision purely based on their perception to invest in the government bond rather than the corporate bond (**D**). However, suppose a tax expert gives the investors information that the after-tax risk premium of the tax-exempt bond is actually higher than the fully taxable corporate bond. The risk-adverse investors will most likely change their decision to invest in the fully taxable corporate bond because this information influences their perception about the bond risk between tax-exempt bond and fully taxable corporate bond.

Another example is, as discussed in the expedient pathway section, people may invest in government treasury bills that are treated as risk free as CDs (**P**). However, the default risks still exit. In the Eurozone debt crisis, Greece's bond has been downgraded to the point it is almost a junk bond, due to the fact that Greek government debt is now 170 % of the country's current GDP (**I**). There are lots of articles about how investors have lost confidence in the Greek bond and believe that there is a high possibility that Greece will default on its government bond. If the investors consider this relevant information and change their perception that not all government bonds are risk free, they will not invest their money in Greece treasury bills to prevent loss.

Therefore, the revisionist pathway differs from the expedient pathway in that it effectively uses information to reshape investors' perception before reaching the final decision, although there may be a degree of incompleteness, noise interference, and interpretational problems. In the area of personal investing, the pathway brings in information to help investors reframe their perceptions to make more wise decision. However, the investing market is very complex. The missing detailed analysis (**J**) here will make the decision not the most favorite one.

Personal Necessity

As indicated in the previous discussion, people also invest in a house, car, education, and retirement. These investments come from our need to better our lives and careers. The first pathway also discussed that when investors have an immediate desire to get a house, they will go ahead and get it no matter how high the interest rate is and whether they have the ability to repay the loan. However, if they evaluate all the available information, they may find that the price of the house is declining all the time and the interest rate is declining too. They may also find that the rent price is declining. Taking this information into consideration, the investors may change their decision to postpone the house-purchasing plan. Some investors will choose to invest in education since they precept education will bring them decent jobs. However, if the additional information tells them that the unemployment rate is increasing and even the graduate students cannot get decent jobs or can only find jobs at a very low pay, they may change their perception and decide not to attend a college right now. Let's also take the retirement plan for example. Investors may think they need to invest in a 401(K) immediately to get a greater amount of retirement fund in the future (**D**) since 401(K) plans are very stable and tax deferred. However, if the financial advisors tell them that 401(K) will not meet their needs due to the high costs, difficult administration, and low contribution, the investors may probably change their perception and decide not invest in the 401(K). However, some information may be inaccurate and misleading. If the investors could not accurately evaluate all the information, the revisionist pathway will lead them to a not-so-favorable investing decision.

Therefore, the revisionist pathway also has its advantage and disadvantage. On the one hand, it can help investors reframe their thinking process and make better decision; on the other hand, the unevaluated information may lead the investors to make bad decisions.

The Value-Driven Pathway

The value-driven pathway builds on the analytical pathway (**I →J→D**) by adding a person's perception to modify the information a decision maker uses in his analysis. With this particular pathway, although the decision maker uses relevant and reliable information in his analysis process, the very information used is shaped by his or her own perceptual framing. As a result, the way the decision maker handles a particular situation is strongly dependent on their own education, training, social, and economic perspective. The decision process is illustrated in Fig. 3.5:

The advantage of this value-driven pathway is that the decision reached agrees with the decision maker's personal preference. Hence, satisfaction on the outcome of the decision will increase. For example, consumers' food purchase today is not just focused on getting the best value out of their spending; they are more concerned with whether the food is healthy for the body. Up to one-half of US adults indicate they would be more likely to purchase a food or beverage product if it provided a health benefit (e.g., prevented heart diseases, boosted their immunity, lowered cholesterol, helped prevent cancer, and/or boosted their energy levels). This

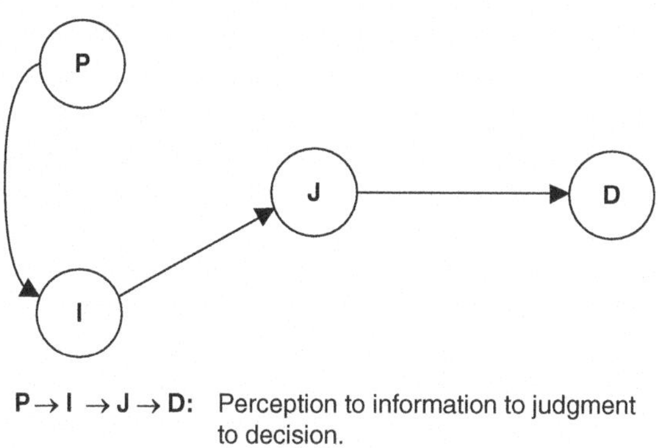

Fig. 3.5 The value-driven pathway

new purchasing trend illustrates that a person's healthy lifestyle will influence the information and analysis used by the consumer in deciding their food consumption.

One clear disadvantage of the value-driven pathway is that it is time-consuming. The analytical process of getting information, weighing information, and performing analysis all take considerable time. When the decision maker is under great time pressure, they will most likely shorten the analytical process and rely on personal perception, ignoring available information sources. Therefore, the decision is oftentimes rushed with an undesirable outcome.

Maximizing Return

When we need to maximize return, we typically invest in stocks. Professional financial advisors popularly advise young people to invest in stocks, and gradually increase their investment in fixed income, such as bonds, as they approach retirement. For example, Fidelity Investment and Vanguard Group both recommend that the fraction of assets invested in equities should increase with one's wealth and decline with one's age. These professional opinions are well informed and well analyzed. Therefore, they could be regarded as the process of **I→J→D** or the analytical process an investor will employ after perceptual framing is formed. If investors are using the analytical pathway process thinking, they will take the professionals' suggestions and investment patterns will agree with the trend that investment in equities increases with one's wealth and decreases with one's age. However, studies have shown that such professional advice contradicts with people's investment behavior (Xie et al. 2010). The observed investment pattern is hump-shaped for stocks. That is, people's investment in stocks gradually increases from young age to middle age, and then goes down. Investment in cash is the opposite: it gradually decreases from young age to middle age, and then goes up.

What causes the discrepancy in people's actual investment pattern and professional's well-analyzed suggestions? Perhaps, personal preference (**P**) is one of the primary reasons for differences in individuals' investment patterns. This professional advice gives little consideration for people's personal needs at different stages of life. Young people hold more cash to prepare for the risk of getting laid off. Since they have just started a job, the risk of losing that job is high and, hence, they have to maintain a high level of cash to hedge against that risk. As people age, layoff risk decreases and, as a result, they invest in more risky assets—stocks. They perceive that their job security is relatively high compared to an entry-level job; hence, they are more comfortable holding less cash and more stocks. As people approach retirement, their job prospects diminish, and they become more risk adverse. Therefore, they hold more cash again. This hump-shaped stockholding over the investor's life cycle illustrates the value-driven decision pathway quite well: job security (perceptual framing) modifies professional advice (information and analysis) to yield a more personalized investment decision.

Minimizing Risk

When choosing a bond, an investor using the analytical pathway will compare return and risk, plus any tax implication to arrive at an optimal choice. However, for the value-driven investor, choosing a bond also involved their personal values and preferences. Even if a bond is proven to be the best one statistically, the investor may choose not to invest in such a bond if the issuer's values do not agree with the investor's personal perception.

Many studies have tried to investigate the role of personal values in an investment decision in controlled experimental settings. Pasewark and Riley (2010) asked their participants to invest in a bond issued by a tobacco company or a bond issued by a non-tobacco company that offered an equal or sometimes lower yield. They surveyed the participants regarding their feelings toward tobacco use to determine whether these values influenced their investment decision. Two factors are highlighted in determining whether participants select a tobacco- or non-tobacco-related investment: the social impact of investment decisions and the health effect of tobacco. They have found that, when the rate of return on a tobacco-related investment exceeds the rate of return on an investment not involving tobacco by 1 %, the concern about social effects influencing investment decisions was especially important. This study has confirmed that socially oriented investors are willing to forgo better investment choices when the company is perceived to be socially irresponsible.

The values supporting fair-trade, resource management and the effectiveness of corporate social responsibility programs are increasingly becoming part of investors' perception of their investment. Corporate Social

Responsibility (CSR) is gradually gaining momentum on how investors view a company and its financial products. Therefore, how investors perceive the company (**P**) will greatly influence the information and analysis (**I→J→D**) process they will employ while making an investment decision. As a result, they may forgo a good investment in a bond if the bond issuer is not socially oriented; or they may accept an investment with higher risk if they determine that the company is using the money wisely.

Personal Necessity

We have seen that personal needs will greatly influence perception, therefore yielding undesirable outcome for investors using the expedient pathway (**P→D**) and the ruling guide pathway (**P→J→D**). Without the help of information, these two pathways may satisfy personal desire at the expense of great financial defeat. However, with the value-driven pathway, a decision maker satisfies personal need through detailed analysis; therefore, they reach the most satisfactory decision with the best return.

Consider a situation in which a family has a child reaching school age and they need to live in a good school district[2]. Their perception (**P**) is simply to give their child the best education; therefore they want to be in the neighborhood of good elementary schools, middle schools, and high schools. Housing prices and mortgage rates (**I**), at the moment, are at a historical low. Therefore, buying a house would be preferred. Yet research (**I**) has shown that house prices in the neighborhoods where the districts for good elementary, middle, and high schools overlap are extremely expensive. Purchasing a house in the good school district will put too much financial strain on the family (**J**). Then the family decides not to purchase (**D**) a house even though the mortgage rate is low and, instead they look for possible rentals. When they take a look at rental prices in the overlapping areas, they find that the rental premiums they have to pay for their child's total school years are less than the purchase premium they have to pay if they decide to purchase a house (**I**). Therefore, the family decides to rent a house (**D**) in the overlapping area until their child graduates from high school and then considers purchasing a more affordable house somewhere else later.

We can see from the previous example that in the value-driven thinking process, investors are going to forsake favorable financial conditions (e.g., affordable price and low mortgage rate) if the offering does not agree with their personal preference (good school district). Perception influences the source of information (i.e., purchasing prices and rental prices). Therefore, different decisions will be reached using this pathway as compared to using the decision pathways discussed previously.

In this section of discussion, we have shown the decision process of **P→I→J→D,** where perceptual framing modifies the information source and, therefore, renders different investment decisions. When making a stock investment, job security at different ages plays an important role in the level of equity holdings. The middle-aged investor holds the highest percentage of stocks, whereas young and retired investors hold more cash. When making a bond investment, corporate social responsibility influences socially oriented investors to the extent that they will accept lower yield if the company is perceived to be socially beneficial. Finally, the decision to buy or rent a house is not solely dependent on the financing terms; rather the investor's personal preference is the determining factor.

In summary, the value-driven pathway may not yield the most financially sound decision overall; yet, it will reach the best decision within the scope of the investor's preference. It will also bring more satisfaction to the investor since the decision is based first and foremost on the investor's individual perception.

The Global Perspective Pathway

The **I→P→J→D** pathway indicates that information sources (**I**) are utilized to update or modify the investors' perception (**P**) before analysis (**J**) begins during a decision choice (**D**) (Rodgers 2006). Under this pathway, the investors are open-minded. The relevant and related information can change the investors' perception before they analyze and reach an investing decision. If there is no time pressure, the investors can take time to search and gather information. What's more, the information should be relevant and reliable. If there is time pressure, it will weaken this pathway because the information may be incomplete and, therefore, affect the final decision. Overall, under this pathway, all the factors are taken into account and, therefore, the possibility that the decision will bring pleasant result is high. Figure 3.6 shows this decision pathway.

The advantage of the global pathway is that decisions are made with an open mind, taking into consideration all the relevant and relative information. Perception is changed or updated based on the given information and detailed analysis is conducted before reaching a decision. Consequently, there is a high possibility the results will be pleasant.

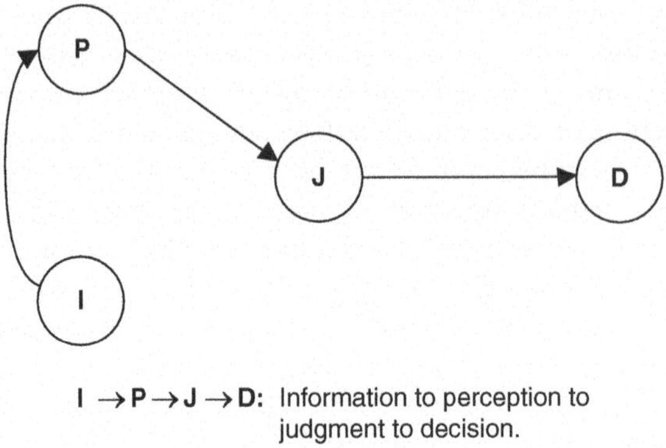

Fig. 3.6 The global perspective pathway

For example, there have been many changes in the accounting principles since 2012. Companies need to gather information (**I**) and make adjustments accordingly (**P**) before analyzing the situation (**J**) and making a decision (**D**). In this way, there is a high possibility the decision will be the right one.

One clear disadvantage of the global perspective pathway is that it is time-consuming, the same as the value-driven pathway. The analytical process of getting information, weighing information, and performing analysis all takes considerable time. When the decision maker is under great time pressure, they will most likely shorten the analytical process and rely on personal perception, ignoring available information sources. Therefore, the decision is oftentimes rushed, resulting in an undesirable outcome.

Maximizing Return

Under the global perspective pathway, investors are likely to consider all the relevant and relative information to update or reframe their perception and then analyze the situation before reaching the final decision. They are more open-minded. Therefore, in the stock market, open-minded investors will take as much relevant and relative information as they can. They not only read the company's financial statement to calculate the financial ratios and understand the company's business and policies, but also tightly observe the company's activities to detect any risk factors. For example, if investors followed the news and articles about Enron a few years ago, trying to get the inside information as well, they may be able to detect the fraud activity of Enron and change their perception that all companies follow the rules. Through this thinking process, losses can be prevented. However, the weakness is that it is extremely time-consuming to search and analyze all the information and situations. The incomplete or interpretation information will weaken this thinking process.

As we also discussed before, stock will bring the investor the highest return along with the highest risk. Considering the risk, the real return on the stock is not high. The average investor in stocks earns just 3.8 % a year. Under the global perspective pathway, investors will seek professional opinions, read news and financial reports, and discuss with friends to get clear idea of the situation. They will rely on their perception and information to expand analysis. They will evaluate the information. If the information is accurate, they will accept the information and reframe their perception. If the information is not accurate, they will continue searching and find accurate and up-to-date information to update their perception. Following this global perspective thinking process, investors will be cautious when putting their money in the stock market. Risk and return will be taken into consideration at the same time to get the maximum return. Perceptions are updated all the time and detailed analyses are always given. Investors will get the most favorable results if utilizing this global perspective pathway.

Let's also take international investing, for example. Since the economy structure and politics in China is totally different from America, the rules that are successfully applied in the American market may not get the same success in China. To be able to get the maximum return on the China market, investors must utilize the global perspective pathway to collect all the relative and relevant information to adjust their perception before any analysis and decision. Although it is time-consuming, it is the best way to get the highest return.

Minimizing Risk

Investors are also very open-minded when their goal is to minimize risk. As we discussed in the Euro debt crisis example, relevant and relative information tells the investors that the government bonds of southern European countries in the Eurozone are downgraded to junk bonds. It's not risk free. There are high possibilities that these southern European countries will default on those debts. Analyzers also doubt that the Eurozone will break to the original status. In this scenario, the rules that government treasury bills are risk free may not apply. Investors must reframe their perceptions and analyze the situation before making any investment decision. Utilizing the global perspective pathway may give them the best results to minimize risk. If they do not apply this global perspective pathway in this changing environment, risk free may become risk taken.

Let's also look at the international market. Investors may apply some hedge strategies to invest money in a different foreign market to minimize the risk. However, transaction risk, economy risk, and translation risk exist in the global market. The environment is changing all the time. It is only under the global perspective pathway that investors fully collect information, including economic and political information. The political information gathered will include not only financial policy but also other relevant policies like environment and energy regulations, since changes in these policies will greatly affect the financial market and trends of cash flow.

Personal Necessity

Investors using the global perspective pathway will consider the relevant and relative information to adapt to the changing environment. As we discussed in the section on the ruling guide pathway, in a stable environment, people tend to invest their money in different areas in different stages of their life. They may heavily invest money in education when they are young since investing in human capital will give them long-term return in the future. However, this rule does not always apply. Let's take Steve Jobs and Bill Gates, for example. Along with the blooming of the Internet, they both dropped out of college and began their entrepreneur venture. If they followed the general rules of life and regularly attended school and postponed their entrepreneur journey until after graduation, they would have probably missed the great opportunities to be the first movers and successful businessmen in the IT industry. Therefore, with open minds and the ability to gather useful information, they modified their perception and bravely embarked on different journeys that led them to success. Similarly, the founder of Facebook Inc., Mark Zuckerberg, quit attending Harvard to run Facebook, the largest social media network in the world. With Zuckerberg's intelligence, knowledge, and open mind, he was able to update and modify his perception and analyze different situations; he designed Facebook to quickly adapt to the fast-changing media environment and became one of the youngest billionaires in the world (see Shayni et al. 2012).

As we also discussed in the previous section, investors who insist on investing in a house in the Northern California real estate market may walk into debt if they do not have the ability to pay off the loans. However, if they consider other relevant and relative information, they will find that with many years of working experience, they could find jobs in Dallas with high paying salaries. Furthermore, not only are house prices in Dallas cheaper than those in Northern California; but, so is education. Therefore, with all the information taken into consideration, the investors will reframe the thinking procedure and will do a detailed analysis, which will lead to a more pleasant decision.

Therefore, the global perspective pathway takes into consideration all types of information that update or revise investors' perception, following by judgment to the final decision. This pathway is an open-minded approach and is the most ideal one among the six decision pathways, if there is no time pressure.

Summary

In conclusion, the six dominant decision-making pathways depicted in this chapter may help assist individual investors in their investment decision choices. These six pathways representing *the expedient pathway, the ruling guide pathway, the analytical pathway, the revisionist pathway, the value-driven pathway, and the global perspective pathway* are one way to relating maximizing returns, minimizing risk, and understanding personal necessities to making decisions. Therefore, the decision-making modeling approach emphasizing personal investments is strengthened by considering the following:

1. an analysis of personal investors' framing of the information (i.e., perception);
2. an analysis of the framing effects on their judgments;
3. the decisions that personal investors make; and
4. feedback designed to help personal investors understand the effects of their investment patterns on their decision choices.

Note

1. See Reuters – Euro zone debt crisis in graphics. Retrieved from http://graphics.thomsonreuters.com/F/09/EUROZONE_REPORT2.html.

References

Frick, Robert. 2011. "How to Be a Better Investor." *Kipling's Personal Finance.* November.

Pasewark, William R., and Mark E. Riley. 2010. "It's a Matter of Principle: The Role of Personal Values in Investment Decisions." *Journal of Business Ethics* 93: 237–53.

Rodgers, Waymond. 2006. *Process Thinking: Six Pathways to Successful Decision Making.* New York: iUniverse Inc.

Shayni, R., A. Das, and J. Letzing. 2012, May 17. Retrieved from http://www.wsj.com/news/articles/SB10001424052702303448404577409923406193162.

Walter, J. (2012). The True Risk of Investing: Understanding the Types of Investment Risk. Retrieved from http://personalfinancewhiz.com/the-true-risk-of-investing-understanding-the-types-of-investment-risk/

Xie, Yan Alice, and Qi. Howard. 2010. "Job Security and Personal Investment Portfolio." *Global Journal of Business Research* 4(1). http://www.icmarc.org/news-and-views/late-career-newsletter/nl-retire-marketview.html.

CHAPTER 4

Residential Real Estate Market Investment Decisions and the Economic Downturn

Abstract This chapter provides an overview of the economic downturn and the process thinking pathways investors most likely used to make bad decisions. Several key factors are introduced, which undoubtedly greatly influenced real estate market investments during this time.

Keywords Economic downturn · Mortgage interest rates · Irrational exuberance

As mentioned previously, the housing bubble in 2006 and the credit crisis in 2008 were the result of millions of Americans' bad real estate investment decisions. This chapter provides an overview of the economic downturn and the process thinking pathways investors most likely used to make bad decisions. We will introduce several key factors, which undoubtedly greatly influenced real estate market investments during this time. Then, we will discuss the six process thinking pathways—*expedient, ruling guide, analytical, revisionist, value-driven,* and *global perspective*—to help us better understand the decisions investors made and how the crises could have been prevented. Finally, we will discuss the historical trends in the residential real estate market that led many investors to believe that buying up houses would continue to be profitable.

W. Rodgers, T.G. McFarlin, *Decision Making for Personal Investment*,
DOI 10.1007/978-3-319-47849-4_4

Economic Downturn

According to the National Bureau of Economic Research, the US economy entered into a recession in December 2007. Indicators of the recession were reflected in the GDP (gross domestic product), the unemployment rate, and the Dow Jones Industrial Average (DJIA) in 2008. Holt summed up the situation as follows:

> Real GDP increased by only 0.4 % for the year 2008, and it decreased at annual rates of 5.4 % in the 4th quarter of 2008 and 6.4 % in the 1st quarter of 2009. The unemployment rate increased from 4.9 % in December 2007 to 9.5 % in June 2009. The Dow Jones Industrial Average (DJIA) reached a peak of 14,279.96 on October 11, 2007, and then fell to 6,440.08 on March 9, 2009, a drop of almost 55 % from the peak.

Economic experts agree that this economic downturn was the worst since the Great Depression. They also agree that the primary cause of this recession was the credit crisis arising from the bursting of the housing bubble in 2006–2007 (Holt 2009). This is because real estate plays an integral role in the US economy (Amadeo 2016). Families depend on residential real estate for housing and it is often the best source of wealth and savings for them. Once the housing bubble burst, values of securities tied to US real estate pricing plummeted, damaging financial institutions globally.

Holt (2009) asserts that the following four factors were the primary cause of the 2006 housing bubble and the credit crisis of 2008: (1) low mortgage interest rates; (2) low short-term interest rates; (3) relaxed standards for mortgage loans; and (4) irrational exuberance, which is defined by Robert Shiller as a "heightened state of speculative fervor."

Low Mortgage Interest Rates

Although, during the housing bubble, the US savings rate was low, mortgage interest rates were kept low due to the influx of saving entering the US economy from investors in other countries, including Japan and China, who sought investments providing relatively low risk and good returns (Holt 2009). These investors first focused on US government securities, then branched out into mortgage-backed securities issued by Fannie Mae and Freddie Mac, two enormous government-sponsored enterprises seeking better returns with low risk, and eventually boldly invested in mortgage-backed securities issued by Wall Street firms that, with favorable ratings from Moody's and Standard & Poor's, appeared to be low risk (Holt 2009). The low mortgage interest rates kept monthly mortgage payments affordable and attracted buyers even as homes prices increased, thereby contributing to the housing bubble.

Presumably, investors relying solely on "interest rates" used the revisionist pathway (I→P→D) to make their decisions. This pathway asserts that investors concentrate on particular sources of information that influence how they frame (perception) home buying (i.e., mortgage payment affordability) in order to make a decision to purchase. There could be other pathways to explain how "low mortgage interest rates" influence decisions, but we believe that the **I→P→D** pathway explains this situation most appropriately.

Low Short-term Interest Rates

The Federal Reserve Board cut short-term interest rates from about 6.5 % to 1 % after the dot.com bubble crashed in 2000 and the subsequent recession began in 2001 (Bianco 2008). Low short-term interest rates encouraged mortgage lenders to offer adjustable rate mortgages (ARMs), which could provide the buyer with a lower monthly payment initially because the short-term interest rates were lower than the long-term interest rates (Holt 2009). For example, a buyer's monthly principle and interest payment on a $350,000 fixed rate mortgage with an interest rate of 5 % would be $1879, while a buyer's monthly principle and interest payment on a $350,000 30-year ARM with an interest rate of 3 % would be $1476.

Mortgage lenders also started offering "option" ARMs that allowed borrowers to make payments of interest only (which resulted in no change to the balance outstanding on the loan each month) or make payments of only part of the interest due (which resulted in the balance outstanding on the loan to increase each month) (Holt 2009). These ARMs, which typically last for 2 years, made mortgage payments seem more affordable for more buyers and consequently played a part in rising home prices. However, when the adjustable rates started to rise, many homebuyers could not handle the higher mortgage payment (Holt 2009).

Secondly, low short-term interest rates encouraged leveraging (investing with borrowed money), which increased the financing available for mortgage lending because investors would borrow at low short-term interest rates and invest in mortgage-backed securities or other higher yielding long-term investments (Holt 2009).

Schiff and Downes (2009) summed it up this way: "ARMs and their variations are a not-so-tender trap to lure people into commitments they can't afford, thus adding impetus to the bubble and accelerating selling pressure on the way down." They also appropriately refer to the ARM as a "time bomb."

In many areas in the United States, especially areas where the highest appreciation occurred during the bubble days, the nonstandard risky loans went from being rare to prevalent (Bianco 2008). In 2004, 80 % of all mortgages originated in San Diego County were adjustable rate and 47 % were interest-only loans (Bianco 2008).

As with interest rates, investors that relied solely on low short-term interest rates also used the revisionist pathway (**I→P→D**) to make their decisions. This pathway asserts that investors concentrate on particular sources of information that influence how they frame (perception) home buying (i.e., mortgage payment affordability) in order to make a decision to purchase.

Relaxed Standards for Mortgage Loans

Several factors led to the relaxing of standards for mortgage loans. These included new governmental policies developed to encourage more lower-income families to become homeowners, increased competition in the mortgage loan market, the increasing securitization of home mortgage debt, and irrational exuberance that overcame everyone involved in the mortgage lending process (Holt 2009).

Traditionally, in the decades before the recent housing bubble started to develop, banks and savings and loan institutions made mostly 30-year fixed rate mortgage loans that would be assets on their books (Schiff and Downes 2009). Lenders wanted to be repaid and, therefore, considered the following before loaning to prospective homebuyers:

1. Creditworthiness and accuracy of property appraisals;
2. *Down payment of at least 20 %*, as insurance that the borrower was not going to walk away from the mortgage or fail to pay on time;

3. *Annual income of the borrower* as banks would not lend more than twice one's annual income.
4. *Total of mortgage payments, interest, and taxes* as this total amount could be no more than a third of pretax income, which was something people could comfortably handle (Schiff and Downes 2009).

One government policy that helped relax these considerations was the Community Reinvestment Act of 1995 (modified from 1977), which pressured lending institutions to increase the number of loans they provided to low-income homebuyers (Whittington 2016). Since many of these borrowers did not have sufficient assets to qualify for a home loan, they were offered what is known as subprime mortgage loans (Whittington 2016). In order to comply with the Community Reinvestment Act, many banks relaxed their conventional mortgage lending standards.

Similarly, Fannie Mae (the Federal National Mortgage Association) and Freddie Mac (the Federal Home Loan Mortgage Corporation), the major government-sponsored enterprises that purchase mortgages from loan originators, had to relax their down payment and income requirements, when, beginning in 1995, the Department of Housing and Urban Development required them to increase their holdings of mortgage loans they had with lower-income households.

The assets Fannie Mae and Freddie Mac acquired became increasingly risky. From 2005 to 2007, they were holding approximately a trillion dollars' worth of subprime and unconventional mortgages, which amounted to roughly 40 % of the value of all the mortgages they bought from lenders (Sowell 2010). According to Ligon and Beach (2013), "By 2010, Fannie and Freddie owned or guaranteed approximately half of all outstanding mortgages in the United States, including a significant share of sub-prime mortgages, and they financed 63 % of new mortgages originated that year."

As the Internet became more accessible to the masses, competition in the mortgage loan market increased (Zandi 2009). Any lender that imposed strict old-fashioned credit standards or had higher mortgage fees would lose business because there were so many other online lenders at buyers' fingertips (within clicking distance) (Zandi 2009).

Mortgage securitization also severely undermined banks incentive to be responsible and imposed strict credit standards. This process involves pooling together individual mortgages with similar characteristics and selling debt securities that draw interest on principal payments from the pool of mortgages, and it allows mortgage originators (banks) to sell mortgage loans from their books and use the money to make more loans (Langsdorf 2016). And that's what a lot of loan originators started doing. Mortgage loans were securitized and sold to investors (investment banks, hedge funds, money market funds, finance companies, asset-backed conduits and structured investment vehicles) and, by the second quarter of 2007, this new system provided $6 trillion in credit, almost as much as the original banking system (Zandi 2009). However, no one was invested enough to care whether a loan was good or not because insurance companies were selling investors credit default swaps (an insurance contract) (Holt 2009). Fannie Mae, Freddie Mac, and Ginnie Mae (the Government National Mortgage Association) are the largest issuers of mortgage-backed securities (Langsdorf 2016).

The relaxed standards enabled a change in the "rules" guiding whatever residential mortgage loans borrowers qualified for. Hence, the ruling guide pathway trumpeted the decision-making process of borrowers, enabling them to qualify for residential loans. This process was very direct and straightforward in that borrowers felt comfortable that they met the banking loan guidelines.

Irrational exuberance over the housing market resulted in its overheating and led mortgage lenders to relax their standards even more. As investment banks bought more mortgages so that they could issue more and more highly profitable mortgage-backed securities, loan originators increased the number of mortgages they sold and had little concern for the long-term credit worthiness of borrowers (Holt 2009).

Irrational Exuberance

Alan Greenspan, chairman of the Federal Reserve Board, coined the phrase "irrational exuberance" in a speech given on December 5, 1996, to describe investor enthusiasm that escalated asset values. Furthermore, Shiller expanded on the subject in *irrational exuberance.* According to Holt (2009), this enthusiasm "played a key role in the housing bubble" as all parties involved in creating the bubble—government regulators, mortgage lenders, foreign investors, insurance companies, and homebuyers—"became convinced that home prices would continue to rise."

Similar to factors (1) low mortgage interest rates and (2) short-term interest rates, "irrational exuberance" is exemplified by the notion that home prices will continue to rise. This type of information presumably influenced how borrowers or potential homeowners framed (perception) their buying decision, thereby leading to the use of the revisionist pathway, which is **I→P→D**.

In addition, the situation referred to as "irrational exuberance" can be explained by the expedient pathway (**P→D**). In other words, some potential homeowners believed (perception) that home prices would continually increase, and they downplayed all available historical information that may have altered or changed their decision choice.

The Glass-Steagall Act

The Glass-Steagall Act, which was passed in 1933 in response to one out of five banks failing after the Great Depression and the stock market crash, forced banks to choose between being a commercial bank or an investment bank and was not well liked from the beginning (Crawford 2011). When it was repealed in 1999, it allowed for the incorporation of commercial banking with investment banking, creating what Stiglitz (2010) refers to as "ever larger banks that were too big to fail. Knowing that they were too big to fail provided incentives for excessive risk-taking" (Stiglitz 2010).

The role the repeal of the Glass-Steagall Act played in the collapse of the American economy is debatable. Some people believe it contributed greatly to the crisis, while others believe it lessened it. One thing is certain, however. Once the Act was appealed, banks began engaging in risky investments in hopes of maximizing returns.

Historical Trends

Before the US housing bubble burst in 2006, recent historical trends led many investors to believe that buying up houses would prove profitable because prices seemingly could not drop. From 1987 to 2005, although there were a few individual quarters when the S&P Case-Shiller home price index fell, the overall trend for that 19-year period was upward. For example, from the 1st quarter of 1990 to the 1st quarter of 1997, home prices increased by about 8.3 (Holt 2009). The increase in home prices was so great that, for the period 1997–2006, the nominal and real returns were

9.7 % and 7.1 %, respectively, and, from 2000 through 2006, the figures were 11 % and 8.2 %, respectively (Swedroe 2012). By the 2nd quarter of 2006, home prices peaked over 132 % higher than they had been 9 years earlier, and, by the beginning of 2009, they had dropped 32 % from that peak, although they were still 57 % higher than they had been in early 1997 (Holt 2009).

As a result of this recent upward trend, the buying and selling process operated like a well-oiled machine. One real estate agent, Mary Laughlin Fenton, summed up her experiences as follows: "Prior to 2006, the market was a frenzy at least in the most coveted neighborhoods. Things moved at breakneck speed. In many transactions, buyers had to be prepared to overbid and have a compelling pitch to spin to the seller. Sellers were in the driving seat if their home was in good condition and in a desired location" (Oliner 2012).

However, all an investor has to do is look at the long-term trend in the US housing market to see a different picture. From 1925 to 1933, US house prices fell 30 %. Additionally, since the late 1970s, house prices have fallen significantly three times relative to the consumer price index (Oliner 2012).

Summary

The bursting of the housing bubble in 2006–2007 and the resulting credit crisis caused the severe recession that began in December 2007. The primary causes of the housing bubble and resulting credit crisis were low mortgage interest rates, low short-term interest rates, relaxed standards for mortgage loans, and irrational exuberance. Each played an important role in creating the housing bubble and credit crisis and the combination of all four made the bubble burst and the resulting credit crisis severe (Holt 2009). The repeal of the Glass-Steagall Act also contributed significantly to the financial crisis. As a result, although the United States had experienced regional housing recessions in recent years, the steep and long-lasting decline in inflation-adjusted home prices in this recession was unprecedented in the post-First World War US economic experience in both severity and geographic scope. All this happened because politicians thought there was a nationwide shortage of "affordable housing," and "set out to solve a national problem that did not exist" (Sowell 2010).

References

Amadeo, Kimberly. 2016. "How Does Real Estate Affect the U.S. Economy? Just a Minor Drop in Home Prices Created the 2008 Crisis." useconomy.about.com. http://useconomy.about.com/od/grossdomesticproduct/f/Real_estate_faq.htm.

Bianco, Katalina M. 2008. The Subprime Lending Crisis: Causes and Effects of the Mortgage Meltdown. http://www.business.cch.com/bankingfinance/focus/news/Subprime_WP_rev.pdf.

Crawford, Corinne. 2011. "The Repeal of the Glass-Steagall Act and the Current Financial Crisis." *Journal of Business & Economic Research.* http://www.unarts.org/H-II/ref/949-3747-1-PB-1.pdf.

Holt, Jeff. 2009. "A Summary of the Primary Causes of the Housing Bubble and the Resulting Credit Crisis: A Non-Technical Paper." *Journal of Business Inquiry* 8(1): 120–29. http://www.uvu.edu.woodbury/jbi/volume8.

Langsdorf, Jonathan. 2016. "What is Mortgage Securitization?" http://homeguides.sfgate.com/mortgage-securitization-2645.html.

Ligon, John L., and William W. Beach. 2013. "Housing Market Without Fannie Mae and Freddie Mac: Economic Effects of Eliminating Government-Sponsored Enterprises in Housing." *The Heritage Foundation*, Special Report #127, January 8. http://www.heritage.org/research/reports/2013/01/a-housing-market-free-of-fannie-mae-freddie-mac.

Oliner, Stephen D. 2012. Booms, Bubbles, and Busts in U.S. Real Estate Markets. *American Enterprise Institute and UCLA Ziman Center.* http://www.aei.org/files/2012/08/06/-stephen-oliner-presentation_092652194301.pdf.

Schiff, Peter D., and John. Downes. 2009. *Crash Proof 2.0: How to Profit from the Economic Collapse.* Hoboken, NJ: John Riley & Sons, Inc.

Sowell, Thomas. 2010. *The Housing Boom and Bust.* New York: Basic Books.

Stiglitz, Joseph E.. 2010. *Freefall: America, Free Market, and the Sinking of the World Economy.* New York: W.W. Norton & Company, Inc.

Swedroe, Larry. 2012. "History Says Home Real Estate is a Bad Investment." *Money Watch*, February 1. http://www.cbsnews.com/news/history-says-home-real-estate-is-a-bad-investment/.

Whittington, Mark. 2016. "The Community Reinvestment Act and the Credit Crunch." *Yahoo Voices.* http://www.voices.yahoo.com/the-community-reinvestment-act-credit-crunch-1992536.html.

Zandi, Mark. 2009. *Financial Shock.* Upper Saddle River, NJ: FT Press.

CHAPTER 5

How the Recent Economic Downturn Differs from Previous Downturns

Abstract This chapter reports on how the recent economic downturn has been different from previous downturns and its effect on mortgage delinquencies, foreclosures, and market recovery. Further, this chapter highlights the process thinking pathways that homeowners used to deal with owing more on their homes than they were worth and examine the trajectory of home values after the downturn.

Keywords Foreclosures · Housing bubble · Market recovery

In this chapter, we will discuss how the recent economic downturn has been different from previous downturns and the effects this has had on mortgage delinquencies, foreclosures, and market recovery. We will also discuss the process thinking pathways that homeowners used to deal with owing more on their homes than they were worth and examine the trajectory of home values after the downturn.

Correction Deeper and More Sustained

When home price appreciation in the United States came to a halt in the summer of 2006, after increasing rapidly in the early years of the twenty-first century, the subsequent downturn in pricing triggered an initial wave of subprime mortgage defaults, which affected the global financial system and eventually brought it to the brink of collapse,

W. Rodgers, T.G. McFarlin, *Decision Making for Personal Investment*,
DOI 10.1007/978-3-319-47849-4_5

thereby paving the way to a deep recession (ERP 2012). By 2009, home prices in the United States on average had declined by nearly 28 % and, in Florida and Nevada by 35–50 %. Although the country had experienced sharp and long-lasting price declines before in previous housing recessions, it had not experienced such a steep and prolonged nationwide decline in inflation-adjusted home prices since the First World War (Economic Report of the President 2012). These conditions made recovery all the more difficult.

Once the bubble burst and home prices started to fall subsequent to poor economic conditions, delinquencies and foreclosures increased tremendously across a broad spectrum of American homeowners (Economic Report of the President 2012). By early 2009, nonperformance rates for prime borrowers increased from to 2.2 % in 2005 to 6.1 % and for subprime borrowers from 10.6 % to nearly 25 % (Economic Report of the President 2012). In other words, approximately 1.7 million homes were in the process of foreclosure and almost 7 % of total mortgage debt was more than 90 days delinquent (Economic Report of the President 2012). In 2010, the delinquency rate was even higher.

More Homeowners Upside Down

The worst of the "housing bust" occurred in 2010. According to CoreLogic, a housing data firm, by the end of 2010, the number of Americans who were upside down or underwater on their mortgages (owing more than their homes were worth) rose to about 11.1 million households or 23.1 % of all mortgaged homes. CoreLogic also indicated that the states with the highest negative equity were Nevada with 65 % of all of its mortgaged properties underwater, Arizona with 51 %, and Florida with 47 %, and Michigan with 36 %, and California with 32 %. Additionally, 2.4 million borrowers had less than 5 % equity in the fourth quarter. Combined, negative equity and near-negative equity mortgages accounted for 27.9 % of all residential properties with a mortgage nationwide (Norman 2011).

During the first part of 2010, the number of upside-down mortgages had fallen. However, this decrease was mostly due to the *increase* in the number of homes that had fallen into foreclosure, a subject that will be discussed further in the next section.

As of the second quarter of 2012, approximately one-third of mortgages in the United States were underwater, according to a report issued by the real estate company (Zillow 2014).

Some homeowners with underwater mortgages often think they have little recourse but continue making payments in hopes the property will eventually regain its value. That is, their perceptions may be optimistically biased in hoping for a drastic change in their fortunes. In this case, the expedient pathway (P→D) helps explain why homeowners may discount or ignore available information about real estate market trends and rely upon their biased perception of how the economy may rebound in the future.

Other underwater homeowners might just refuse to sell their homes at a loss because of biased perceptions, which ignore information sources or sound judgment, or they may not be able to get the lender to agree to a short sale (selling the property for less than the amount owed on the mortgage). Moreover, they might attempt to refinance their mortgage but probably won't qualify, since most lenders demand that you have at least 20 % ownership (equity) in your home in order to refinance your loan.

Other homeowners with upside-down mortgages may decide to stop making payments and allow the lender to foreclose, which could be the most rational thing to do when a homeowner is more than 10–15 % upside down on a mortgage. Some financial experts refer to this as a "strategic" or "ruthless" default. However, in terms of process thinking, these homeowners are using the analytical pathway (I→J→D) to decision making; they are maximizing their overall welfare by reasoning with information and judgment. The idea here is not to look at foreclosure as a personal failure but rather as a correction in the market that homeowners cannot control. It is not the end of the world, nor does it have to be the end of homeownership. One formula for long-term homeownership is to (a) stop making payments on an upside-down mortgage and let the property go; (b) save for a down payment on another home; (c) repair credit; (d) buy back into the market at an appropriate price; and (e) build equity.

It is interesting to note here, however, that, while the analytical perspective (**I→J→D**) suggests that increasing homeowners' overall economic value is the goal, the global perspective pathway (**I→P→J→D**) suggests that real estate decisions should be influenced by considerations beyond economics. This pathway supports the notion that other factors, such as spouse's and children's relationships developed in the neighborhood, should be dominant factors when considering foreclosure options.

Foreclosure

By 2010, US foreclosures hit a new record high due to a catastrophic combination of homeowners' financial hardships (joblessness and decreased wages) and strategic default, either voluntary (to unload upside-down mortgages) or involuntary (the result of failed loan modifications). According to a 2010 year-end foreclosure report produced by RealtyTrac, the leading online marketplace for foreclosure properties, there were a total of 3,825,637 foreclosure filings (default notices, scheduled auctions, and bank repossessions) reported on a record 2,871,891 US properties that year, an increase of nearly 2 % from 2009 and an increase of 23 % from 2008. One in 45 US households (2.23 %) received at least one foreclosure filing during the year. This reflects a steady increase in foreclosures since 2006, when the percentage was 0.58 % foreclosures (RealtyTrac 2011).

In 2011, the number of foreclosures climbed even higher to 3,920,418 and it was estimated that foreclosure filings may jump 20 % from the record in 2010. However, this did not happen. The number of filings increased only by 2 % and, in 2012, foreclosures decreased considerably.

Foreclosures Drive Down Home Values Further

Foreclosures drive down home prices for two reasons. One, they add to the housing supply. Two, the financial firms that acquire the properties want to unload them as soon as possible. Research conducted by MIT economist Parag Pthak and two Harvard researchers, John Y. Campbell and Stefano Giglio, concluded that foreclosure reduces home value by 27 %, on average (Dizikes 2010).

Incentive to Foreclose

Unfortunately, banks and other lenders have more financial incentive to let borrowers lose their homes through foreclosure than they have to work out settlements with them. Although the government currently requires lenders to have loan modification programs in place, under the Making Home Affordable Plan, and provides subsidies to lower mortgage payments for distressed borrowers, there is no law that requires lenders to actually modify loans, and lenders are not guaranteed to profit by doing so. They only profit if, after the loan modification, the borrower can sustain the more modest payments (Merle 2009).

Trajectory of Home Value Trend

According to the Case Shiller Index (Division Street Capital 2016), the cyclical low point for housing prices nationwide seems to have occurred in February 2012 and prices for the twenty largest metropolitan areas have increased by 2.0 % from August 2011 to August 2012. While this increase is not big, it shows an upward trajectory, which Kenneth Rosen, chairman of the Fisher Center for Real Estate and Urban Economics at the University of California, Berkeley, predicts should continue at 1 or 2 % more than the inflation rate for several years (Mullins 2010).

However, not all big cities in the nation experienced an upward trajectory of housing prices in early 2012. Chicago, for example, did not hit bottom until the end of 2012 when median house values went down 38 % (Zillow 2014), after a downward trajectory for six straight years. Factors that kept Chicago home prices depressed included the city's huge backlog of bank-owned properties and other properties near foreclosure (5 % in 2012); lenders' tightened credit requirements; and young people's tendency to rent rather than buy a home after seeing prices drop and friends go through foreclosure or a short sale.

Summary

After the housing bubble burst in the summer of 2006, the decline in home prices was steeper and more prolonged nationwide than any other decline since the First World War. More homeowners than ever were negatively impacted. Mortgage delinquencies and foreclosures increased tremendously and steadily and, by the end of 2010, over 23 % of all mortgaged homes were upside down or underwater. Many of these upside-down borrowers strategically defaulted on their mortgage payments, thereby adding to the foreclosure filings, for which lenders had little incentive to reduce with loan modifications. It was not until February 2012 that housing prices nationwide started to recover.

References

Division Street Capital. 2016. Housing Market Data. http://www.divisionstreetcapital.com/housing-market-data.html.

Dizikes, Peter. 2010. How Foreclosures Hurt Everyone's home Values: MIT Economist Measures How Much Foreclosures Lower Housing Prices. http://web.mit.edu/press/2010/housing-prices.html.

Economic Report of the President. 2012. Chapter 4, Stabilizing and Healing the Housing Market. http://www.whitehouse.gov/sites/default/files/microsites/ERP_2012_ch_4.pdf.

Merle, Renae. 2009. "Foreclosures are Often in Lenders' Best Interest." *Business*, July. http://www.articleswashingtonpost.com/2009-07-28/business/36893209_1_borrowers-michael-fratantoni-lenders.

Mullins, Luke. 2010. "The Future of Home-Price Appreciation." March 4. http://www.money.usnews.com/money/personal-finance/real-estae/articles/2010/03/04/the-future-of-home-price-appreciation.

Norman, Dennis. 2011. Number of Homeowners Underwater on Mortgage Increases. http://stlouisrealestatenews.com/real-estate-market/number-of-homeowners-underwater-on-mortgage-increases/.

RealtyTrac Staff. 2011. "Record 2.9 Million U.S. Properties Receive Foreclosure Filings in 2010 Despite 30-Month Low in December." January 12. http://www.realtytrac.com/content/press-releases/record-29-million-us-properties-receive-foreclosure-filings-in-2010-despite-30-month-low-in-december-6309.

Zillow. 2014. In Most Major Markets, Negative Equity Has Fallen By Half Since Peak of Crisis. http://zillow.mediaroom.com/2014-12-17-In-Most-Major-Markets-Negative-Equity-Has-Fallen-By-Half-Since-Peak-of-Crisis.

CHAPTER 6

The Real Estate Market Investment

Abstract This chapter examines real estate investment from the homeowner's perspective and conducts a comparative analysis of the rent option. It also explores when renting might be the better option. Finally, this chapter illustrates the investment component of the residential real estate investment.

Keywords Appreciation · Leverage · Cash flows · Real estate investment

In this chapter, we will take a look at real estate investment from the homeowner's perspective, conduct a comparative analysis of the rent option, and explore when renting might be the better option. We will also discuss the investment component of the residential real estate investment.

From the Homeowner's Perspective

To homeowners, the typical real estate market investment is quite simple. There are upfront costs and ongoing carrying costs and benefits. Upfront costs are usually one-time payments that are incurred when a home is initially purchased. These include a down payment of at least 3–5 % of the selling price and closing costs associated with the loan. Although the closing costs vary depending on the lender and the buyer's offer, they cover such things as an appraisal, home inspection, credit check, insurance, and assurance that the title to the home is free (O'Hara 2007).

W. Rodgers, T.G. McFarlin, *Decision Making for Personal Investment*,
DOI 10.1007/978-3-319-47849-4_6

Ongoing carrying costs include one's monthly mortgage payment, property taxes (which are based on the value of the home), home insurance, maintenance, and homeowner association (HOA) fee, if applicable. Mortgage payments are deductible on income taxes if itemization is utilized. Property taxes are also tax deductible.

The HOA fee is a "hidden" cost that must be paid monthly by owners of certain types of residential property, including condominiums and single-family houses in certain neighborhoods where there are common amenities like tennis courts, a community clubhouse, or neighborhood parks to maintain. This fee generally covers costs for city services such as trash removal, water, and sewage; insurance for damage to the outside of the building and surrounding property; lawn care; pest control; and maintenance and repairs to the outside of the complex. It could possibly increase from year to year as the costs of services go up. Additionally, the homeowners association may levy special assessments on occasion when there are insufficient funds in the HOA's reserve to cover major repair, such as a new roof or a new elevator. And, if owners do not pay the required monthly fee and any special assessments, the homeowners association has the right to foreclose on the delinquent homeowner.

Prospective homebuyers typically consider all these costs and conduct a comparative analysis of other options in the marketplace before making a decision to buy a specific property. They should also consider whether buying is the best option for them.

Comparative Analysis of the Rent Option

Since the housing bubble burst in 2006, more economists and real estate experts have taken to the Internet with comparative cost analyses to advise skeptic consumers whether it is better to buy or rent property in today's economy. One of the simplest calculations presented is the price-to-rent ratio (P/R ratio) or the rent ratio. A more complex analysis is Trulia's methodology, which was developed by the online real estate marketplace known as Trulia (Kolko 2013). Both analyses make the decision to buy or rent a purely financial decision.

Price-to-Rent Ratio

Checking the P/R ratio is done by finding two similar properties, one for sale and the other for rent, and dividing the sale price of one property by the annual rent for the other property (Roth 2012). For example, if one finds a house he or she would love to buy for $400,000 and also sees that a house around the corner is renting for $2000 per month ($24,000 a year), dividing $400,000 by $24,000 would give one a P/R ratio of 16.7. According to David Leonhardt, Washington bureau chief of the *New York Times*, when the rent ratio is below 15, most people should consider buying and when the ratio is above 20 one should definitely consider renting because a high ratio means the monthly mortgage bill will be higher than renting a similar property (Leonhardt 2011).

Although the national P/R ratio is usually between 10 and 14, during the recent housing bubble, the ratio came close to 20 and, in some cities, went far above (Roth 2012).

Trulia's Rent vs. Buy Methodology

In a 2013 *Forbes* article, Jed Kolko, chief economist at Trulia, indicated that, based on Trulia's methodology, "homeownership is (still) 44 % cheaper than renting in the top 100 major metros." This methodology involves calculating the following:

1. the average rent and for-sale prices for an identical set of properties over a period of time;
2. initial total monthly costs of owning and renting, including maintenance, insurance, and taxes;
3. future total monthly costs of owning and renting, considering price and rent appreciation and inflation;
4. one-time cost and proceeds, such as closing costs, down payments, sales proceeds, and security deposit; and
5. net present value to account for opportunity cost of money (Kolko 2013).

Trulia's method also assumes buyers put 20 % down, get a 3.5 % fixed rate mortgage for 30 years, reside in the 25 % tax bracket, itemize their federal tax deductions, and live in the home in question for at least 7 years (Kolko 2013).

For example, the calculated results for ten metropolitan areas are based on where buying a home is much cheaper than renting. The negative numbers indicate that it is cheaper (i.e., 70 % cheaper) to buy than to rent (Kolko 2013). The higher the negative number, the more sense it makes to buy property.

When Renting Might Be Better

Using Trulia's methodology, renting becomes the better option, when mortgage interest rates are higher than 3.5 %, buyers do not itemize deductions, and they do not plan to live in the same place for more than 7 years (Kolko 2013).

Renting is also the better option when one is looking to buy in a seller's market, in which case demand for homes exceeds the supply of homes for sale and those on the market sell quickly, which can drive up home prices. In this particular situation, the prospective homebuyer ought to make an offer promptly to the seller. Further, the prospective homebuyer has little room to negotiate with the seller since the seller has numerous offers to choose from.

Investment Component of Residential Real Estate

While some Americans struggle today with the decision whether to buy or rent a primary residence, others are looking to purchase residential real estate strictly for the purpose of generating income. They do not plan to live in the property or use it as a vacation home. The investment property is usually bought with the intent to either rent it out or renovate it to resell at a profit, although a primary residence can become an investment property in the event the owner needs to move but does not need to sell. Financial gains for real estate investments include cash flow, appreciation, and leverage.

Cash Flow

Cash flow from real estate investments is the excess of rental receipts after subtracting expenses of operating and owning the property. If one invests in quality real estate, cash flow should increase over time (Benchmark Group).

Appreciation

Appreciation refers to an increase in the value of the property and is only realized through selling or refinancing the property. Appreciation rates vary depending on regional and economic situations such as employment rates, interest rates, business growth, housing supply, demand, and affordability. The rates also vary depending on crime rate in the neighborhood, weather, quality-of-life issues, and the quality of schools and other factors, including home upgrades.

Leverage

Financial leverage, also known as trading on equity, is the use of debt (financial instruments or borrowed capital) to acquire additional assets. It is most commonly used in transactions through the use of a mortgage to purchase a home and increases the potential return of an investment. For example, if Harry purchases a home by investing $300,000 of his own money and borrowing $500,000, he is controlling real estate valued at $800,000 while having only invested $300,000 of his own money. If the property increases in value by 25 % and is sold for $1 million, Harry will gain $200,000, which is a 66 % return on his investment. Real estate investors who "flip" properties thrive on these returns. However, there is a flipside to the gains. If the value of the property decreases, then Harry, like all other Americans with upside-down mortgages, stands to lose money if he sells the property.

With this in mind, some may decide to invest in stocks or bonds rather than in real estate. The stock market has high risk and high volatility, in addition to being massively unpredictable, but offers the opportunity for quick return. Bonds are another source for investing in real estate. They offer a low, stable return with minimized risk. However, inflation can destroy earnings.

Summary

People purchase homes to either live in or profit from. When deciding to buy a home to live in, there are several things to consider, including upfront costs, ongoing costs, and the benefits of buying a home versus renting. To assist prospective homebuyers with this decision, there are various comparative cost analyses they can use, including the P/R ratio and Trulia's rent vs. buy methodology. The analysis Trulia conducted in 2013 shows that home buying is still 44 % cheaper than renting in the top 100 metropolitan areas, as long as interest rates stay below 3.5 % and buyers itemize deductions and plan to live in the same place for more than 7 years. When planning to invest in property for profit, investors need to consider possible cash flow, appreciation, and financial leverage.

References

Kolko, Jed. 2013. "Buying a Home Still Cheaper." March 20. http://www.forbes.com/sites/trulia/2013/03/20/rentvsbuy-winter2013/.

Leonhardt, David. 2011 "Rent or Buy, a Matter of Lifestyle." May 10. http://www.nytimes.com/2011/05/11/business/economy/11leonhardt.html?_r=0.

O'Hara, Shelley and Nancy D. 2007. *Complete Idiot's Guide to Buying and Selling a Home*. New York: Alpha Books.

Roth, J.D. 2012. "Is It Better to Rent or Buy?." December http://www.business.time.com/2012/12/03/is-it-better-to-rent-or-to-buy/.

CHAPTER 7

Irrational and Rational Homeowner Considerations

Abstract This chapter covers how homeowners and marginal borrower's irrational decision making using the *expedient* or *revisionist* pathway affected the housing market and what pathway they should have used to make more rational decisions in the real estate market. Real estate transactions examined in this chapter include the home equity loan, cash-out refinancing, and loan modifications.

Keywords Irrational real estate decisions · Expedient pathway · Revisionist pathway

In *Crash Proof*, Schiff and Downes remind readers that the American dream is to go from rags to riches by working hard and saving money and has nothing to do with owning a home. They see the "misconception of the dream and the importance given to home ownership" as a force that drove the housing bubble and affected the policies dealing with the bust (Schiff and Downes 2009). The US government drove this force. In 1993, the Department of Housing and Urban Development started taking legal action against mortgage bankers who denied more minority applicants than white applicants for mortgage loans. From then on until 2000, federal officials increasingly pressured lenders to relax lending standards so that people who would not ordinarily be eligible for mortgage loans would qualify (Sowell 2010). Lenders responded by lowering down payment and income requirements (Sowell 2010). Consequently, from 2000 to 2007,

W. Rodgers, T.G. McFarlin, *Decision Making for Personal Investment*,
DOI 10.1007/978-3-319-47849-4_7

many Americans took advantage of the expansion of mortgage credit, and, by 2006, approximately 5 million marginal borrowers owned a home that they would not have owned had it not been for the credit boom (Mian and Sufi 2014). The extension of credit triggered rising home prices, which had an effect on existing homeowners who saw rising home equity as a way to finance home improvements and consume more (Mian and Sufi 2014). Then, when the housing bubble burst and home prices started to fall, homeowners who were substantially upside down in their properties tried to secure loan modifications to stay in their homes. Most economists agree that the decisions homeowners and prospective homeowners made during that time were as irrational as the decisions made by federal officials and lenders. Using Rodgers' six major pathways for decision making, it is obvious these decisions were made using the expedient pathway, where perceptual bias plays a dominant role.

In this chapter, we will discuss how homeowners and marginal borrower's irrational decision making using the expedient or revisionist pathway affected the housing market and what pathway they should have used to make more rational decisions in the real estate market. Real estate transactions that will be examined along the way include the home equity loan, cash-out refinancing, and loan modifications.

Irrational Real Estate Decisions Using the Expedient or Revisionist Pathway

As discussed in Chap. 2, the expedient pathway or revisionist pathway for decision making is the least time-consuming way to make a decision and the riskiest (Rodgers 2006). The decision maker relies heavily on his or her perception, which is influenced by education, cultural background, and personal emotions, and gives little consideration to available information (Rodgers 2006). During the housing boom and bust, the expedient pathway became the dominant thinking process for homeowners and prospective homeowner's financial decisions, as they got caught up in the "irrational exuberance" ignited by lenders and investors. Homeowners who borrowed equity from their homes via home equity loans or cash-out refinancing during the boom, marginal borrowers who purchased property for the first time when credit was expanded to them, and homeowners who sought loan modifications after the housing bubble burst all let emotional considerations drive their decisions and ignored reliable and relevant information that could have saved them considerable expense in the long run. Home equity borrowers, driven by the irrational belief that house prices would continue to rise, were determined to maximize return on their investments. Marginal borrowers, driven by the misconception of the "American dream," were determined to achieve a personal necessity (owning a home). And loan modification-seekers, driven by irrational emotional attachment to their homes and antiquated notions of meeting commitments with lenders, were determined to keep their personal necessity at any cost.

To better understand how the expedient pathway affected homeowners and prospective homeowners' decisions, let's look at each of the real estate transactions separately.

Home Equity Loans

A home equity loan provides cash proceeds to homeowners based on the equity (ownership amount) they have built up in their home (Homeloan.com). It is basically a second mortgage secured by the homeowner's property (Pritchard 2016). This loan appeals to borrowers because they can borrow relatively large amounts of money and it is easier to qualify for than any other type of loan. Additionally, the home equity loan usually has a lower interest rate or Annual Percentage Rate (APR), interest cost that is tax deductible and low or no closing costs or other fees (Justin 2016).

From years 2002 to 2006, US homeowners borrowed so aggressively against the rise in home equity over half of the increase in debt for homeowners came from home equity loans. This aggressive response to house price increases significantly fueled the house-debt crisis in the United States (Mian and Sufi 2014). Surprisingly, however, homeowners with low credit scores (below 660) borrowed more aggressively than those with high credit score (Mian and Sufi 2014). Research shows that for every $1 increase in home-equity value, they borrowed approximately $0.40 cents and they spent the money mostly to consume more and improve their homes (Mian and Sufi 2014). Home equity loans nearly doubled during this period, going from a total of $593 billion in 2003 to $1.3 trillion in 2007 (Sowell 2010). Although this may seem rational to some people, many of these individuals had substantial credit card debt outstanding with high interest rates and they did not use any of the money extracted to pay down this debt, nor did they use any of the funds to purchase a new home or invest in another property (Mian and Sufi 2014).

Those who had bought and paid for their homes prior to the housing boom borrowed much more than they paid for their houses because they based their borrowing on the house's rising value during the boom (Sowell 2010). For example, if during the housing boom, a house that was bought in 1992 for $90,000 was worth $600,000, the homeowner could easily take out a $250,000 home equity loan on the home. While this may not seem problematic to some people, imagine a couple who, back in 1959, purchased a two-bedroom home for $11,500 and then had to foreclosure years later because their child refinanced the property several times and now the family owes over $400,000 (Sowell 2010).

The elderly also sought home equity loans and were offered what is known as a "reverse mortgage." This is a loan that does not require any repayment. Part of the equity is just transferred to the lender who holds it until the borrower dies and then turns it into cash at that time (Sowell 2010). During the housing boom, these loans increased considerably (Sowell 2010). In 2001, there were less than 8000 reverse mortgages while, in 2005, there were more than 40,000 (Sowell 2010).

In a 2004 *Fortune* magazine article, readers were warned not only that housing speculation was quickly "losing touch with reality" but also that the growing practice of borrowing against home equity was a risky business. The article summed up the situation as follows: "there's a real danger that a downturn in prices, or even a stall, could slam the economy, especially all important consumer spending. Americans have used their homes like ATMs, taking out $662 billion in home-equity loans and refinancings since 2001" (Sowell 2010).

Cash-out Refinancing

Cash-out refinancing, another form of the home equity loan, became very popular during the housing boom (Sowell 2010). Typically, when a homeowner refinances, he or she receives a new first mortgage and the existing home loan is eliminated (HomeLoan.com). The new loan usually has a lower interest rate than the previous mortgage and/or more favorable terms, such as a fixed rate rather than an adjustable rate. In cash-out refinancing, the new mortgage also includes the equity, which the borrowers get in cash (Amisano and Media 2016). Sowell gives the following example:

> Someone owing $300,000 on a mortgage with a fixed interest rate of 8 % could take out a new loan to replace the old loan when the interest rate fell

to 6 %. But instead of taking out another $300,000 mortgage loan at 6 %, the homeowner could take out a $400,000 loan at 6 %, paying off the existing mortgage loan from the proceeds of the new loan and keeping $100,000 in cash.

The lower interest rate often results in a borrower's monthly payment remaining the same, even though the mortgage was larger (Sowell 2010). Consequently, during the housing boom, the number of loans in this category rose significantly. In 2000, homeowners pulled a total of $26 billion out of their refinanced mortgages to spend as they pleased, while, in 2006, they pulled out $318 billion (Sowell 2010). "Cash-out" refinances made up 86 % of the more than six million home mortgage refinances in 2006 (Sowell 2010). Homeowners were not dissuaded from refinancing when most housing markets in the United States started to weaken in 2006 (Jurow 2010).

Lenders are required to report to the federal government under the Home Mortgage Disclosure Act (HMDA) (Jurow 2010). We can see "how total refinancing soared in 2002 as the Federal Reserve drastically lowered interest rates to minimize the economic fallout from 9/11" and how "refinancing in 2003 was simply off the charts" (Jurow 2010). We can also see how refinancing dropped to slightly less than 8 million originations in 2004. However, it is important to note that, according to Freddie Mac, approximately 40 % of the refinancing that occurred in 2004 was cash-out refinancing (Jurow 2010). According to real estate analyst Keith Jurow (2010), this was the year "when home prices really soared, by 30–40 % in the hottest bubble markets" and "cash-outs began to take off."

Marginal Borrowers and Credit Expansion

Prior to the credit boom, those individuals who could not secure mortgage credit—marginal borrowers—were renters. The mortgage application denial rate in areas with the worst credit scores (below 660) was 43 % compared to the denial rate of 16 % in areas with the highest credit scores (Mian and Sufi 2014). However, from 2002 to 2005, the availability of credit in low credit-score areas increased considerably. The increase led to 30 % more accepted mortgage loans per year in low credit-score areas until 2007, when more and more homeowners started to default on their loans and lending requirements tightened again (Mian and Sufi 2014).

The mortgage loans offered to the marginal borrowers with low credit scores and little or no down payment are known as subprime mortgages. These mortgages have higher interest rates than conventional loans, which are offered to borrowers with FICO scores 660 or above. If the loan was made on the basis of income information that was not verified, "stated income," then the interest rate was even higher, sometimes several points above traditional loans. Most subprime mortgages are also adjustable-rate mortgages (ARMs). Popular subprime loans were the option ARMs, also known as the 2/28. Features of the option ARM included the following:

- a fixed rate for 2 years;
- rate changes and fluctuations every 6 months for the next 28 years, with a 2 percentage point change beginning in the third year;
- cap rate of 6 points over the initial rate;
- prepayment penalty, which made refinancing more costly (Weintraub 2016).

Marginal borrowers irrationally accepted these subprime loans, when they should have put emotional considerations aside and paid attention to the warning signs that they were being duped by lenders. Economist Joseph E. Stiglitz summed it up this way:

> It was well known that the financial sector was engaged in all of these shenanigans, and it should have been a warning to borrowers, to the investors who bought the mortgages, and to the regulators. They all should have seen that mortgage origination was fee-driven: the borrower had to constantly refinance, and at the point of financing there were new fees—large prepayment penalties in settling the old mortgage and further charges at the issuance of the new mortgage. The fees could be recorded as profits, and high profits generate high share values for the mortgage originators and others in the financial sector.

The irrational reaction of marginal borrowers to the expansion of mortgage credit contributed to the astronomical increase in household debt in this country from 2000 to 2007; during these seven years, household debt actually doubled, rising to 74 trillion (Mian and Sufi 2014).

Loan Modification

A loan modification is an adjustment to the terms of a homeowner's existing loan by the lender. It may involve lowering the borrower's interest rate, reducing the principal balance of the loan, extending the length of amortization, and/or changing loan type (e.g., from a variable rate to a fixed-rate loan). Loan modification differs from refinancing in that the adjustment to the loan is usually temporary to assist the homeowner during a difficult time or through an unexpected hardship; however, the original loan is still in place (mortgageloan.com). Borrowers tend to seek loan modifications when they do not qualify to refinance their mortgage due to a low (below 620) credit rating (mortgageloan.com).

The problem is nearly all homeowners interested in loan modification are substantially "upside down" or "underwater" in their property. And, as economists Mian and Sufi point out, "underwater households are much more likely to default on their mortgage payments, either because the payment becomes prohibitively expensive or because of strategic motives." Therefore, it makes little sense to modify the terms of mortgage loans to help borrowers who are behind with payments when there is a good chance they will default on the loan later (Sowell 2010). For example, in 2009, the *Economist* magazine reported the following: "Of 73,000 loans modified in the first quarter of 2008, 43% were again delinquent eight months later" (Sowell 2010).

Emotional considerations influenced homeowners to seek loan modifications rather than default on their loans, even though, in some cases, default would have been a strategic move rather than a forced move. Defaulting generally has a negative connotation and borrowers did not want to feel irresponsible, shamed, or helpless.

However, lenders often played hardball with those seeking loan modifications. Below are four examples of homeowners who sought assistance from the law firm of McFarlin LLP to secure loan modifications.

Example 1

Farmers operating a dairy farm out of their home entered into a forbearance agreement with a lender after falling behind on their mortgage payments. Generally, a forbearance agreement is an agreement to postpone, reduce, or suspend loan payments for a designated limited amount of time. In this case, the forbearance agreement involved loan payment reduction. Based on information (**I**) from the lender, it was the farmers' understanding (**J**) that the lender would permanently modify their mortgage after the completion of the forbearance agreement. The farmers, in other words, made the decision to sign the agreement using the analytical pathway (**I→J→D**). However, after they completed the forbearance agreement, the lender refused to modify their home loan and proceeded to foreclose on their home. Hence, apparently, the convenience of information was not complete in terms of reliability.

McFarlin LLP filed a lawsuit against the farmers' lender, contesting the nonjudicial foreclosure process and breach of the forbearance agreement. After the law firm obtained a temporary restraining order from the court, the lender offered the farmers a loan modification, which included over $500,000 in principal reduction.

Example 2

Homeowners Josie and Gerald F. were struggling to make their mortgage payments, as a result of mounting medical bills and loss of employment (I). Seeking relief, they perceived (P) that a loan modification would allow them to continue making monthly payments and keep their home. However, when they discussed the loan modification process with their lender, they were informed that they needed to become delinquent on their mortgage payments in order to qualify and be approved for any loan modification. This new information modified their perception, which, in turn, influenced their judgment (J) about making payments, and they became delinquent (D), as the lender advised. In other words, these homeowners viewed the loan modification process from a global perspective (**I→P→J→D**). However, after becoming delinquent, their lender refused to modify their mortgage.

McFarlin LLP filed a lawsuit against the lender, contesting the nonjudicial foreclosure process and false representations made by the lender. And, after obtaining a temporary restraining order from the court, the lender offered the plaintiffs a loan modification, which included over $330,000.00 in principal reduction.

Example 3

Joseph L. obtained a negative ARM loan with a lender, but was not informed that the rate on his loan would adjust. When it did, his mortgage payment increased from $750 per month to over $2,100 per month. Consequently, he contacted his lender and requested that his rates not be reset. The lender told him he must become delinquent in order to qualify for any loan modification. Mr. L. did what the lender told him to do; he became delinquent. As a result, his lender refused to modify his mortgage. Apparently, Joseph L. implemented a revisionist pathway (**I→P→D**), since the lender information was "valid" and not taken as a key factor from the loan agreement for analysis (judgment) purposes.

Again, with the help of McFarlin LLP, Mr. L. filed suit against his lender, contesting the nonjudicial foreclosure process and false representations made by his lender, and the lender finally offered Mr. L. a loan modification, which included a substantial reduction in the interest rate on the loan.

Example 4
Mary J. was a homeowner who also struggled to make her mortgage payments as a result of the economic downturn. Seeking relief, she tried to obtain a loan modification from her lender for over two years but the lender continuously gave her the runaround. Then the lender finally told her that in order to qualify for a loan modification, she had to become delinquent on her payments. As with the previous examples, Ms. J. became delinquent, her lender refused to modify her loan, and she was at risk of losing her home.

McFarlin LLP brought suit against her lender, contesting the nonjudicial foreclosure process and false representation made by the lender, and, after obtaining a temporary restraining order from the court, the lender offered Ms. J. a loan modification, which included a significant reduction in the interest rate on her loan.

Rational Homeowner Considerations

During the housing boom and bust, homeowners and prospective homeowners would have experienced more cost savings had they used the analytical, revisionist, or global perspective pathway to decision making rather than the expedient pathway because these pathways involve making decisions with the aid of information. As mentioned in Chap. 2, the analytical pathway is one in which an individual identifies and analyzes all factors and alternatives before choosing the optimal alternative (Rodgers 2006); the revisionist pathway "highlights an unstructured environment in which one may use all available information to influence perception before rendering a decision"; and the global perspective pathway "is where information adjusts one's perception that leads to judgment, then to a decision choice" (Rodgers 2006).

Homeowners who borrowed equity from their homes or refinanced them should have considered the following:

1. **Underwater Risk**. When homeowners borrow too much of home equity, they can end up underwater. The maximum amount to borrow should always be carefully calculated. Borrowers should do their homework. Rather than taking advice from lenders and loan brokers, they should research and analyze what real estate experts and economists are saying about the market today and what they are forecasting for the future.
2. **Possibility of Home Loss.** Home equity loans and refinance loans involve using one's home as collateral. Therefore, if something unforeseen happens in the borrower's life and he or she is unable to make the loan payments, the lender has the right to take one's home and sell it so that it does not incur a loss.
3. **Closing Costs and Fees**. Although these vary depending on the type of loan program one is offered, they can add up.
4. **Repayment Terms**. Borrowers should never overestimate their ability to pay off the loan quickly with high payments. They should consider all of their other financial obligations and factor in expenses that they know they will be responsible for in the near future. This is personal information at their fingertips. Therefore, there is no reason they should be making decisions without considering this. Borrowers may have the perception that they will be earning more money next year and want to include this in their process thinking, but other financial obligations are *real* and should not be underestimated.
5. **Teaser Rates Concealing Long-run Costs**. Teaser rates are interest rates "charged during the early months of a new mortgage" that were below even the unusually low interest rates being charged on mortgages in general during the housing boom. The unusually low initial monthly mortgage payments, made possible by the temporary "teaser" rate, would then be followed by higher monthly mortgage payments when the prevailing interest rate replaced the teaser rate—followed still later by another increase in monthly mortgage

payments when time came to begin repaying the principal on the mortgage loan (Sowell 2010). "During the height of the housing boom in 2005 and 2006, an estimated 15 % of adjustable–rate mortgages that were issued had initial interest rates below two %" (Sowell 2010). Borrowers should always consider whether they can afford to make the loan payment at its highest rate.

6. **Low Interest Rates/Balloon Payments**. While it is important for homeowners to obtain the lowest interest rate possible when borrowing equity from their home or refinancing, this information alone is not enough. They need to consider the other terms of the loan before making a decision. An interest rate may be low because a balloon payment is due a few years into the loan or it is an interest-only loan.
7. **Credit Score Affect on Loan Costs**. Although this may seem like a no-brainer, during the housing boom, some borrowers of home equity did not question (analyze) loan cost information as their primary concern was maximizing return on investment by borrowing against home equity. Waiting three to six months before applying for a home equity loan or cash-out refinancing could have made a considerable difference in some borrowers' lives as their credit scores may have been higher. As a rule, one should always keep credit card balances low, carrying no more than 30 % of one's available credit on any card.
8. **Private Mortgage Insurance.** Lenders may require this, if your current mortgage and what you are planning to borrow add up to more than 80 % of your home's value.
9. **Choice of Mortgage Broker.** During the housing boom, there was a lot of predatory lending going on. Homeowners should research brokers before doing business with them to make sure they are experienced and ethical.
10. **Comprehension of Loan Documents.** Lastly, homeowners should make sure they fully understand what they are signing. If they do not understand, they should get a lawyer or an analytical friend to review the documents before signing anything. According to Sowell, there are "indicators" that many "less sophisticated home buyers may not have fully understood how much their monthly payments could rise under adjustable rate mortgages with initially very low interest rates and sometimes an initial period of perhaps two years when they were paying only interest on their mortgage loan" (Sowell 2010).

Marginal borrowers should have considered the following before purchasing homes when credit was expanded to them:

1. **Closing costs and fees.**
2. **Repayment terms.**
3. **Teaser rates concealing long-run costs.**
4. **Credit score effect on loan costs.**
5. **Choice of mortgage broker.**
6. **Comprehension of loan documents.**
7. **Carry costs** (mortgage, taxes, insurance, utilities, upgrades, deferred maintenance, the cost of lawn upkeep or landscaping) of owning a home versus the cost of a comparable rental.
8. **Opportunity costs.** These are the costs of paying more than the cost of a comparable rental.
9. **Mortgage affordability.** Some prospective homeowner failed to acknowledge their own financial limitations before purchasing a home. They should have honestly asked themselves whether they could really afford the home they desired.

Homeowners who sought loan modifications after the housing bubble burst should have considered the following:

1. **Carry costs.**
2. **Opportunity costs.** When homeowners are upside down in a property, they should seriously reconsider their home investment because that money could be used elsewhere where it could possibly generate greater and more reliable returns. The best economic option would be to move into a rental property that is more affordable and save money for the next big real estate boom to recover current losses, unless it is projected that the time frame to return to an equity position is going to be short as indicated below.
3. **Estimated time frame for an upside-down Home to return to an equity position.** When a homeowner is upside down on their mortgage but the time frame for the home to be upside down is projected to be relatively short, then he or she should probably consider applying for a loan modification rather than foreclosure, which not only drives down the value of neighbors' homes and does not help in the recovery of the real estate market, but could negatively affect one's credit score for several years.

4. **Upside-down threshold.** When a homeowner is 20 % or more upside down on his or her mortgage and there is no short time frame projected for the home to be upside down, he or she should consider foreclosure or options for avoiding foreclosure, which will be discussed in the next chapter.

Summary

As Schiff and Downes indicated in their book *Crash Proof*, "getting rich by owning a home is not the American dream, or at least it was not the original American dream." From 1993 to 2000, the US government inflated the importance of homeownership by taking legal action against mortgage bankers who appeared to discriminate against minorities who applied for mortgage loans and then pressuring lenders to relax lending standards. Once lenders responded to this pressure by lowering down payment and income requirements, many American renters/marginal borrowers irrationally took advantage of the expansion of mortgage credit, which resulted in rising home prices and homeowners irrationally borrowing home equity through home equity loans or cash-out refinancing. And, when the housing bubble burst, some homeowners continued to behave irrationally by seeking loan modifications rather than walking away from properties they could not actually afford. All of this irrational behavior stems from the fact that, during this time, marginal borrowers and homeowners made important real estate decisions using the expedient pathway for decision making, which is the quickest way to make a decision but the more risky. They relied heavily on their perception of the opportunity before them and gave little consideration to available information, such as closing costs and fees, repayment terms, teaser rates concealing long-run costs, underwater risk, etc. They, in other words, underestimated risk and would have made better decisions had they used the analytical, revisionist, or global perspective pathway, all of which consider information as an important piece of the decision-making process. In *Freefall*, economist Joseph E. Stiglitz states that the government "has an important role to play: it should not only prevent the exploitation of individual irrationalities but also help individuals make better decisions" by taking action (monetary, fiscal, and regulatory) to help stabilize the economy (Stiglitz 2010). However, knowledge is power. Individuals should always arm themselves with information and not wait for the government to protect them from unscrupulous lenders and mortgage brokers.

References

Amisano, Chris and Demand Media. 2016. Differences between Home Equity Loans and Refinancing.

Jurow, Keith. 2010. Special Report: Is Massive Refinancing During Bubble Years a Ticking Bomb? http://www.worldpropertyjournal.com/us-markets/residential-real-estate-1/real-estate-news-mortage-refiancing-real-estate-bubble-fdic-financial-crisis-inquiry-commission-president-obama-home-equity-lines-of-credit-heloc-2633.php.

Justin, Pritchard. 2016. Home Equity Loans: The Basics of Home Equity Loans. About.com Banking/Loans. http://banking.about.com/od/loans/a/homeequity/loans.htm.

Mian, and Sufi. 2014. *House of Debt*. Illinois: University of Chicago Press.

Rodgers, Waymond. 2006. *Process Thinking: Six Pathways to Successful Decision Making*. New York: iUniverse Inc.

Schiff, Peter D., and John Downes. 2009. *Crash Proof 2.0: How to Profit from the Economic Collapse*, 2009. New Jersey: John Riley & Sons, Inc., Hoboken.

Sowell, Thomas. 2010. *The Housing Boom and Bust*. New York: Basic Books.

Stiglitz, J. E. 2010. *Freefall: America, Free Markets, and the Sinking of the World Economy*. New York: W.W. Norton.

Weintraub, Elizabeth. 2016. How Soon Can We Buy a Home after a Short Sale or Foreclosure? http://homebuying.about.com/od/foreclosures/f/071008_BuyAgain.htm.

CHAPTER 8

Foreclosure and Options for Avoiding Foreclosure

Abstract This chapter highlights that the six dominant decision-making pathways can definitely assist us in selecting the best pathway that can eliminate or reduce uncertainty as well as provide us, when necessary, the insightful means of problem solving. This chapter examines foreclosure and foreclosure options available to borrowers who wish to walk away from a property.

Keywords Deed-in-lieu of foreclosure · Short sale · Pre-foreclosure equity sale

Although there was less foreclosure activity nationwide in the first half of 2014 since before the housing bubble burst in August 2006, foreclosure continues to be an issue in some states and local markets. This is partly due to the fact that correction of the residential real estate market continues to be slow, despite the massive improvement in home prices. Although 312,000 homes in the United States regained positive equity in the first quarter of 2014, approximately 6.3 million homes or 12.7 % of all residential properties with a mortgage were still with negative equity (upside-down mortgages), and approximately 10 million (20.6 %) of the 43 million homes that have equity have less than 20 %. Borrowers with less than 20 % equity are almost as bad off as those with no equity as they oftentimes have a hard time refinancing

W. Rodgers, T.G. McFarlin, *Decision Making for Personal Investment*,
DOI 10.1007/978-3-319-47849-4_8

their homes, obtaining financing to buy another home, and/or covering the down payment necessary to purchase another home. Consequently, some of these borrowers are choosing to walk away from their properties. As mentioned in Chap. 4, sometimes foreclosure is the right economic decision for a borrower after careful analysis (process thinking) of one's situation.

In this chapter, we will discuss foreclosure and foreclosure options available to borrowers who wish to walk away from a property. We will also provide real-life examples for each option to show in which situations they may best be utilized and explore how to buy another home after taking such drastic measures.

Foreclosure

Foreclosure is the legal right of a lender to take ownership of a property when a borrower stops making payments on the mortgage loan. The foreclosure process is lengthy. A borrower who defaults on loan payments will first receive a warning from the lender in the form of a "Notice of Default" and then a grace period during which time he or she must make arrangements with the lender to either pay the outstanding amount owed or sell the property for less than is owed, which is known as a "short sale" (mcfarlinlaw.com). If the borrower cannot or will not pay the outstanding balance and no one buys the house during the short sale period, the property will be auctioned off to the highest bidder. However, the borrower can still stop the foreclosure by paying off the outstanding amount. If the borrower does not stop the foreclosure and the property does not sell at auction, the lender will take ownership of the property and get a real estate agent or liquidation auction to sell it.

Options for Avoiding Foreclosure When Walking Away

Although there should be no shame in foreclosure, there are options for borrowers who are 20 % or more upside down on their mortgage loans and decide to walk away from their property. These options include the following:

1. deed-in-lieu of foreclosure;
2. short sale; and
3. pre-foreclosure equity sale.

Borrowers and homeowners can obtain assistance with these options through (1) the Making Home Affordable Program, which is the federal government's plan "to help homeowners avoid foreclosure, stabilize the country's housing market, and improve the nation's economy" (makin ghomeaffordable.gov); (2) Hope Now, which is a voluntary alliance of nonprofit counselors, mortgage companies, investors, and other mortgage market participants; or (3) legal representation experienced in foreclosure law.

It is important to note, however, that these options can be complicated solutions and they must be negotiated properly. Consequently, it is advisable for homeowners to seek legal counsel. The benefits of having legal representation far exceed the cost. In terms of process thinking, the attorney will provide the homeowner with relevant and reliable information about foreclosure and foreclosure options and assist him/her in analyzing (judging) the homeowner's situation and making a decision to resolve the perceived problem (upside-down mortgage).

Deed-in-lieu of Foreclosure

This is a process in which the borrower agrees to give back ownership of the property to the lender, and the lender agrees to forego foreclosure proceedings. Borrowers who owe much more than their property is worth and want to walk away from it tend to like this option because, in many cases, the lender can be persuaded to waive any "deficiency" (loan amount left unpaid) after the property is sold (mcFarlinlaw.com). However, most lenders have strict requirements and qualifications for a deed-in-lieu of foreclosure and the process can take a long time. Therefore, as mentioned above, it is best to have legal representation with this option (mcfarlinlaw.com).

Short Sale

A short sale occurs when a lender allows a borrower to sell a home for less than the mortgage liens on the property before the foreclosure process is completed. The borrower is responsible for finding a buyer for the property and the lender or an authorized agent must approve of the sale. Once the lender approves the short sale, the borrower pays no deficiency. However, the Internal Revenue Service (IRS) could treat the difference between the selling price and the short sale price as income, unless directed otherwise.

Consequently, any homeowner considering this option should consult with a tax advisor or work with a short sale attorney (mcfarlinlaw.com). The short sale must be structured correctly in order for the borrower to avoid owing additional taxes.

Following is an example of a short sale McFarlin LLP successfully negotiated.

Example 1

Marvin G. was having trouble in making his mortgage payments after his employer reduced his work hours and took away his opportunity to work overtime. When Mr. G. sought relief from his lender, he was approved for a trial plan agreement that reduced his monthly payments. Pursuant to the trial agreement terms, Mr. G. was supposed to make his first three payments and then the bank would modify his mortgage payment to a lower amount. However, after he made the first three payments, the lender refused to abide by the agreement to modify Mr. G's mortgage as promised.

Mr. G. contacted McFarlin LLP and they, in turn, filed suit against the lender, contesting the nonjudicial foreclosure process and breach of the forbearance agreement. The lender then offered Mr. G. a loan modification. However, after careful legal analysis of the situation, a loan modification did not seem to be the best solution to Mr. G.'s problem. His home was over $200,000 underwater and it did not make any financial sense for him to hold on to it. Therefore, an agreement was secured from the lender to allow Mr. G. to complete a short sale.

When Mr. G. first came for legal advice to secure a loan modification, he was using the value-driven pathway to decision making (**P→I→J→D**); he allowed his perception to modify and select the information used in making that decision, downplaying the fact that he was $200,000 underwater. After consultation with my firm, he was able to see the global perspective and make a better decision.

Pre-foreclosure Equity Sale

This is when a borrower has been delinquent on payments and the lender accepts less than is owed on the property to settle the loan. It differs from a short sale in the degree of delinquency. With short sales, a borrower may have had only one or two late mortgage payments.

Buying a Home after Foreclosure or Foreclosure Option

When a borrower forecloses on a property or takes advantage of one of the foreclosure options discussed, he or she can expect a significant reduction in their credit score. A foreclosure or a deed-in-lieu of foreclosure can result in a credit score drop between 250 and 280 points. A short sale can result in a credit score drop between 80 and 100 points.

However, the good news is one can still buy a home after the experience and after a waiting period, which is generally as indicated in Table 8.1.

During the waiting period, there are several things one should do to increase the chances of securing the best home loan possible.

1. Reestablish credit by ensuring all bills are paid on time.
2. Routinely monitor credit score with the goal of raising one's score above 650.
3. Ensure stable employment.
4. Reduce monthly costs and save enough money to provide at least a 5 % down payment.
5. Adopt the mindset that a monthly mortgage payment should be no more than 40 % of your monthly income, after factoring in home insurance and taxes.
6. Prepare to explain why you took the action you did.
7. Research lenders to see which ones will more easily qualify you for a home loan. Veterans Administration (VA) and Federal Housing

Table 8.1 Waiting periods for buying another home

Option	*Waiting period*
Foreclosure	5–7 years
Foreclosure (with extenuating circumstances)[a]	3–5 years
Deed-in-lieu of foreclosure	4–7 years
Deed-in-lieu of foreclosure (with extenuating circumstances)[a]	2–7 years
Short sale	1–2 years
Pre-foreclosure equity sale	1–2 years

[a]Extenuating circumstances include death of spouse, illness, job transfer, and injury resulting in disability (Weintraub)

Administration (FHA) are usually willing to offer good fixed rate loans to those who have gone through the short sale process.

8. Three months before looking for a property, get pre-approved for a mortgage loan.

Summary

Understanding the six dominant decision-making pathways can definitely assist us in selecting the best pathway that can eliminate or reduce uncertainty as well as provide us, when necessary, the insightful means of problem solving. This chapter examines foreclosure and foreclosure options available to borrowers who wish to walk away from a property. In addition, this chapter offers real-life examples for each option to show in which situations they may best be employed and discover how to buy another home after taking such drastic measures.

Reference

McFarlin LLP. Retrieved from http://www.mcfarlinlaw.com/.

CHAPTER 9

Conclusion

Abstract People are faced with investment decisions all the time. Many of them are not even aware of it. There are many different ways to invest money: purely stock or bond investment, portfolio investment or CD savings; domestics investment or international investment; personal necessities such as house investment, education investment, or retirement investment. In the new century, investment opportunities occur every day and everywhere. Process thinking helps investors to know when and how to combine perception, information, and judgment to reach a good decision. It also assists us in selecting one of the six pathways to be more confident in making decisions.

Keywords Investment decisions · Investment opportunities · Decision making

Decision making is a vital part of personal financing and investment choices. As we discussed in the introduction section, people are faced with investment decisions all the time. Many of them are not even aware of it. There are many different ways to invest money: purely stock or bond investment, portfolio investment or CD savings; domestics investment or international investment; personal necessities, such as house investment, education investment, or retirement investment. In the new century, investment opportunities occur every day and everywhere. The environment is changing rapidly

W. Rodgers, T.G. McFarlin, *Decision Making for Personal Investment*,
DOI 10.1007/978-3-319-47849-4_9

nowadays, especially with technology and globalization. To improve the quality of personal lives, we must select the most appropriate pathway to reach the optimum investment decision.

Process thinking helps investors to know when and how to combine perception, information, and judgment to reach a good decision. It also assists us in selecting one of the six pathways to be more confident in making decisions.

The expedient pathway (**P→D**) is mostly utilized when investors are faced with greater time pressure to make a decision. That is, when it comes to investing, time pressure is really an issue in the option of stock market. Therefore, we do not recommend investors utilize this pathway to make financial decision.

The ruling guide pathway (**P→J→D**) takes consideration of judgment. Investors make investing decisions using their internal or external rules. This pathway sometimes may be effective and efficient in a stable environment. However, today the environment is changing rapidly. Changes in regulations and rules increase the chance of fraud activities. Ignoring relevant and relative information will lead investors to make unpleasant decisions.

The analytical pathway (**I→J→D**) is grounded on the availability of information to conduct a detailed analysis before reaching a decision. It is useful to minimize risk such as bond investing. However, in the stock market, stock prices today depend on speculations of future performance of the stock. We can gather all relevant and reliable information on past performance; however, we do not know the future performance of the stock. This pathway assumes that all the information is accurate and the environment is stable and controllable. However, the stock market is unstable and a lot of factors cannot be predicted or controlled.

The revisionist pathway (**I→P→D**) combines information and perception. Relevant and relative information will update or modify investors' perception before reaching a decision. However, missing judgment in this pathway will allow the investors little time to analyze all the information. Therefore, if all the information taken is relevant, relative, and correct, it will be helpful for the investor to make a decision when time pressure is great. However, if the information is biased and incomplete, it will lead investors to unsatisfactory decisions. In personal investment decisions, we do not recommend this decision pathway.

The value-driven pathway (**P→I→J→D**), perceptual framing, modifies the information source and, therefore, renders different investment decisions. Investors at different ages choose different investing alternatives. The determining factor using this pathway is the investor's personal preference, which will result in an investment decision that is not the most financially sound but one that is the most satisfying to the investor since the decision is based first and foremost on the investor's individual perception.

The global perspective pathway (**I→P→J→D**) is the most ideal pathway among all the six decision-making pathways. It takes into consideration all types of information that updates or revises investors' perception and then is followed by judgment before the final decision is made. In stock investments, investors utilize the global perspective pathway to collect all the relevant and relative information to reframe their perception. They are open-minded. Detailed analysis will also follow the reframed perception before final decisions are made. Investors will not only examine the financial reports, auditors' opinions, news articles, and experts' opinions, but also closely observe the companies' activities and the change in the regulations. In this way, their perception can be reframed timely and a more favorable decision can be made in the rapidly changing stock market. Similarly, in the bond market, investors utilizing this pathway will better control all the risk factors to minimize default risk and economic risk. In dealing with personal necessities, with an open mind, investors could absorb all information to update their perception to seek a better life. However, the global perspective pathway and the value-driven pathway are both very time-consuming. If time pressure is too great, incomplete or misinterpreted information will weaken these two thinking processes.

In sum, decision making in personal financing and investments is vital since there are consequences to making the wrong decision. When individual investors are making decision choices, it is important that they weigh their options since poor choices can result in painful legal, financial, or personal issues.

To make better decisions, individual investors can start by defining which of the six dominant pathways is appropriate for the situation. Defining a particular pathway removes distractions that are irrelevant to the decision choice. Once personal investors have a clear understanding of the appropriate decision-making pathway, they can determine alternate ways of approaching the problem. Implementing the best alternative is always the course of action, but the best alternative may look different depending upon the decision-making pathway one selects for problem solving. After implementing a particular pathway, individual investors can better measure, monitor, track, and implement their decision choice to ensure they consistently make wise decisions.

Index

W. Rodgers, T.G. McFarlin, *Decision Making for Personal Investment*,
DOI 10.1007/978-3-319-47849-4

The manufacturer's authorised representative in the EU is Springer Nature Customer Service Centre GmbH, Europaplatz 3, 69115 Heidelberg, Germany. If you have any concerns regarding our products, please contact ProductSafety@springernature.com

Printed and bound by CPI Group (UK) Ltd, Croydon, CR0 4YY
22/09/2026
02221070-0004